Me 'n God in the Coffee Shop

Renè Donovan

First printing January 1998
by Book World, Inc./Blue Star Productions
ISBN-13: 1-881542-49-1
Cover photograph by Donovan Photography
Author's photo on back cover by Marjorie Perry

Second Printing:
Copyright © 2015 by Renè Donovan
Published by: Enchanted Cottage Publishing

All rights reserved. This book or any portion thereof may not be reproduced or used in any manner whatsoever without the express written permission of the author, except for brief quotations or for a book review.

Also by Renè Donovan
The Daughters of Time
The Stone Children

Communicate with the author
http://www.dream-scapes-art.com
rdonovan38@comcast.net

Page 135: "The Tao of Physics," Fritjof Capra. A Bantum Book published by arrangement with Shambhala Publications, Inc., 1976. Reprinted with permission by Fritjof Capra.

*This book is dedicated to my son Mark—
this is my new lullaby*

*and to my daughter Katrina—
my rainbow connection.*

Chapter 1

The Dreamtime

I met them in the Dreamtime. Ahh, the Dreamtime, that openness where we travel in imagination, that drifting, shifting veil of dreams and visions. It echoes of our past, whispers of our future.

Yes, the Dreamtime in which our ancestors traveled the path of the Way...those shamans, prophets, seers and seekers who opened the door to approach the God, the Goddess. What awaits us when we rip that veil which has kept us bound to matter is a Creator that is our friend, who throws back His/Her head and laughs in bubbling, overflowing joy.

What? You ask if this Dreamtime is real? Oh, my friends, can you see the wind, the atom, a thought? Though invisible to our eyes are they less real? Oh, yes, the Dreamtime is with us, reaches out to us, touches us feather-soft, whispers simple truths. Quiet, shhh, listen...

And now, my fellow world-mates, leave the stress and bewilderment that overwhelms our planet today. Open your hearts and travel with me on a journey to the Dreamtime.

Once upon a very recent time there was a little coffee shop in a little town on the coast of New England...

The homey aroma of coffee and bacon greeted me as I walked into the coffee shop and sat at an empty booth where the morning's sunshine spread patches across the Formica tabletop. I barely had time to shrug out of my jacket when the waitress set a big mug of steaming coffee in front of me. It was a substantial mug like the ones you used to get in diners: white, rounded, compact, heavy. It was a serious cup, one that meant business. It spoke of the strong, dark brew within which satisfied that morning coffee craving. It was a cup filled with nostalgia for a time when a cup of coffee cost twenty-five cents. I took a tentative sip then pulled my notebook and pen from my big leather purse and opened to a fresh page. I always carried a notebook for those emergency flashes of insight, for hopefully brilliant musings, to make never-ending lists of things to do and sometimes to just complain. Today it was the latter I began to catalog.

I grumbled about life in general: why did it have to be so hard, why so unfair, so violent? Why couldn't we keep a wonderful Christmas feeling all year? During the month of December there seemed to truly be goodwill among humankind but on the day after our New Year celebration when the lights are removed from windows, when the tree is stripped, discarded and the dried needles swept up, when the music we've enjoyed on our stereos is silenced along with cheerful holiday greetings to friend and stranger alike we surrender the magic. So easily and so willingly we trudge back to dull existence. Is it possible to wake every morning with a thrill of expectancy?

On and on I wrote, drinking coffee and scrawling in my almost illegible handwriting, pausing finally when the waitress refilled my cup. My eyes lifted from my notebook-world and I observed the people seated at the circular counter, some in self-imposed privacy of newspapers others eating, drinking and chatting. Listening to several people in an animated conversation I realized they were feeling the same negativity as I and asking the same questions.

One elderly man the others called George was talking about the morning's chilling newspaper headline, "Bloody Night in Boston!" He shook his head in despair and said, "When I moved here...it's goin' on almost fifty years now, I never locked my doors when I left the house. Nobody did. Now I lock up when I'm *in* the house. Gets worse every year."

A woman two seats from him folded her newspaper and nodded. "I listen to the TV news every night because I feel I should know what's going on in the world but sometimes I wonder why I bother. I can't change anything and I get so depressed and frightened." She patted the newspaper as if trying to settle the issue, then continued, "Four murders in Boston last night, all kids, just *kids* killing each other over drugs. Last week it was a boy killing his parents and younger brother and sister and that wasn't a poor or deprived child. He came from an affluent family. The boy had everything. Why on earth would he do something like that?" Her careworn face was turned toward George, sad eyes imploring him for an answer.

"Connie," George began, "don't you see? If a kid really has

everything he *wouldn't* do such things. It ain't necessarily money that keeps a kid from going wrong."

Another voice joined in, this coming from a barrel-chested man wearing a denim jacket, his black hair curling over the collar, dark eyes on George as he spoke. "My heart goes out to the parents of these kids. How can you know these days if you're doing it right or not? There's so much out there to get a kid in bad trouble...drugs, alcohol, AIDS, guns in *school* for God's sake." He ate the last bite of toast, wiped his mouth on his napkin and shoved his plate away. "I'm glad mine are grown and on their own. I don't think I could cope with raising kids today."

George nodded and said, "When my wife was alive, sometimes we'd get all gussied up and go into Boston for a night on the town. Oh, we'd have a grand time...go out to dinner, see a play maybe...that kind of thing. I wouldn't go in now if you paid me. Shame too, I used to really enjoy that but it's not just here, you know and it's not just in big cities. It's all over now, even in places that used to have the lowest crime rates. Lord, I'm almost eighty years old and I've seen a lot but I never thought I'd live to see such goings-on. I'll be damned if I know what the answer is." George sipped his coffee and scowled.

Well, I thought, this is cheery. A little visit to the Diner of Despair. It was definitely one of those days. You know what I mean? A day when a black cloud hovers, dropping big blobs of Bad JuJu onto your life. It occurred to me that perhaps I'd better change my attitude or this darkness would follow me all day, like some oozing disease.

My attention returned to my notebook with the intention of writing in a more positive vein when I felt a presence, someone standing very close to me, exuding a kind of warm energy. The expression *"like a breath of fresh air"* came to my mind because what emanated from him was April winds, new mown grass, autumn leaves, pine forests. I looked up into a face of smiles. It was a face one seldom encounters, one very old yet, the eyes, the eyes were as clear and curious as those of an infant. There was a radiance about him that I had never experienced in another human being.

He smiled and I found that, despite feeling drawn to him, I wished that he'd leave. He was...what? Too much, too vital, too blissful, too attentive. His beaming face was disconcerting. Go away, I thought, but he didn't go and the warmth from his body and the radiation in those eyes held me.

Bending down close to me he whispered, "What are you writing?" His voice was rich and warm as sunshine.

I shivered. Oh, God, what's happening. I didn't want to talk with this person. Why did I feel such anxiety while at the same time feeling so drawn to him? He reminded me of someone. Who? Ah, yes, Walt Whitman, the poet. If I didn't know that he died in the late 1800s I would have sworn this was Whitman. Even the clothes he wore were the style I'd seen in his photographs: wide-brimmed hat dipped jauntily over one eye and covering long, gray silky hair, white long-sleeved linen blouse open at the throat, dark pants of a heavy material and scuffed leather boots. His complexion was ruddy, his gray beard and mustache were full, eyes clear and sparkling and, while everything about him spoke of manliness, there was a feminine gentleness in his manner and grace. Emanating from him, surrounding him like an aura was that comforting aroma of nature: sea salt, autumn leaves, earth, campfire, new mown grass. He seemed the embodiment of the forest, the seashore, the mountains.

Unable to speak I simply shrugged, pulled my eyes from his and looked at my notebook, not seeing what was written there but trying to focus on anything other than his eyes, eyes that were mesmerizing. He sat in the seat opposite me, folded his big hands together and, leaning on his elbows, softly questioned, "Does it help?"

I frowned and glanced up at him. "Does what help?"

Pointing at my notebook, he answered, "Writing."

Again I shrugged, then nodded, "Sometimes. It's like therapy, I guess."

"Well," he beamed, "good for you!"

I laughed despite my misgivings. It was like having a conversation with Santa Claus, he seemed so jolly and delighted with life.

"Oh, much, much better," he declared, creases blossoming on his face as his smile deepened. "Your laughter on this beautiful morning is just what this world needs."

I sipped my coffee then said bluntly, "I don't think my laughter is going to make a damn bit of difference in this world."

"Oh, but you're wrong! Oh, my, yes! It can all begin," he whispered, his hands unfolding as if offering a gift, as if setting free a dove, "with *joy*!"

Oh, jeez, I moaned to myself. Here we go. *A nut!* I always attracted the strange ones. I could be in a crowd of millions and if there was one psychopath, one lunatic who fancied he was Napoleon or Elvis he'd head straight for me and want to be my pal. Just yesterday, for instance, a woman sidled up to me in an almost vacant parking lot and informed me that she'd just seen a German Shepherd driving a truck and wouldn't you think people would know better than to let their pets drive. I, of course, agreed.

He tilted his head, observing me as though amused, his long gray hair falling to one side. "What?" he smiled. "You fear me because I speak of joy? Joy is creation itself. Joy is God, Goddess."

A *religious* fanatic! The worst kind of lunatic. They never get insulted, they don't leave, they just keep trying to *save* you. I knew it! It's those charismatic, charming ones who end up being cult leaders, mass murderers, people who commit unspeakable acts. Walt

Whitman, indeed. More like Son of Sam, Jim Jones, Drakula, even.

He threw his big head back and laughed until tears streamed from his eyes. Picking up a napkin he dabbed at his eyes and between chuckles, choked out, "Drakula...oh, that is amusing, so amusing. Son of Sam..." and the laughter began again.

I stared at him astonished. I wanted to get up and run out to my car and go anywhere that was not here, anywhere safe. The man was reading my mind and the man was crazy! But some unnamable thing kept me in my seat, my mouth open in horror. The laughter that so consumed him stopped abruptly and, as if in slow motion, I watched his hands reach out to mine. Before I could withdraw, his big hands encircled mine. His face was filled with compassion and a love that was beyond anything human.

"Oh, my dear one, not for anything would I ever want to frighten you. Sometimes my delight in people just overwhelms me."

That touch. Those hands encircling mine. My mind was whirling, confusing thoughts and emotions battling to come to some sane conclusion of this experience. Then, as he continued to hold me, as I looked into his eyes, a peace began to fill me, a calm that was beyond anything I'd ever experienced. I felt I was *becoming* him, uniting with him, losing myself. I blinked my eyes, yanked my hands from his and slid out of the booth, spilling my coffee as I reached for my notebook and purse. I dared not even glimpse him as I hurried out the door, almost running to my car.

Once inside the car, I locked the doors and drove away, headed toward the ocean, always my refuge. After a short time, I slowed my speed, rolled the window down and breathed deeply. There has be an explanation, I kept thinking, but he *can't* be just a crazy old man. All those feelings I experienced. They were real. Why would I feel so drawn to him? I know the Crazies like me but I've never returned those feelings. I mean, when someone looking remarkably like Charles Manson saunters up to me on the subway I do as any reasonably intelligent person would do. I walk away slowly and find someone really big to stand beside. I do not chat with them, I've never invited one home and have never allowed one of them to hold my hands and gaze into my eyes. You have to quickly draw a line with these people without blatantly offending them.

In fifteen minutes I turned onto the dirt road leading to the ocean, parked my car and walked down a grassy hill, over a little wooden footbridge and through a path between tall, dry seagrass, finally emerging onto a sandy beach. The tide was low and all was quiet save for the rustle of the wind in the seagrass and the cries of the gulls as they fed where the receding tide had exposed mussels, crabs and other small sea creatures.

Slipping out of my sandals I walked by the water, the cool sand under my feet reminding me that, despite the blue clarity of the cloudless sky and the warm wind, it was still spring and New England's beaches would not be really warm until June. I walked to where a small rowboat had been pulled up onto the beach and sank beside it, resting my back against it's rough wood. The sun was soothing and I let my mind drift back to my experience in the coffee shop. In my mind's eye I saw that face, heard him whisper, "It can all begin...with *joy.*"

Drifting, drifting, I followed each word he had spoken, saw again his wonderful face, could smell the clean aroma that surrounded him but surely, surely he hadn't read my thoughts. I *must* have spoken aloud. I've got to get out more, socialize a bit. Being in only my own company so much was tipping the scales of my psyche into dangerous territory. After a while I opened my eyes, retrieved my notebook from my purse and began to write all I could remember of the encounter. Finished, I capped my pen and smiled. God, I thought, why did I get so upset? He was just a harmless old man, probably lonely and seeking company. The rest had to be just coincidence. My own feelings of fear? Considering the negative frame of mind I was in and the conversation I'd just eavesdropped upon about the "Bloody Night in Boston!" no wonder I was a bit overemotional.

I felt so much better having written of the incident and exhaled a deep breath, allowing the sun and the oceanside sounds to soothe me into a semi-sleep. Still, his words echoed—joy, joy! Images of joy curled behind my eyes, shapes and emotions that I have lived and loved: the silky, chubby bodies of my babies held against me, making love by the ocean on a hot, summer night, witnessing the appearance of a double rainbow over the rising sun. Joy—sudden, spontaneous, heart-swelling, eye-sparkling. When do we lose it? When did life get so serious that it is only a grinding struggle to survive? These images and questions flowed on this lazy Saturday morning until I stretched like a cat, breaking the sun's hypnotic spell. I slowly sat up, arms encircling my knees, and gazed at the sun-dappled scene before me of ocean, gulls and clouds now forming on the horizon.

This was just what I needed. A time out, a breather to see what that negative place can do to me. Oh, the negativity is so quiet, so stealthy. It slides in on cat's paws and filters into the mind and before you consciously realize it you're caught up in the spiral and your entire world is woven in muddy colors. I'll be more careful, I resolved, not to let the nightly news and other people's negativity get to me.

From a distant place in my mind, like an echo emanating from a tunnel I heard his words, "You fear me because I speak of joy?" No, I thought, I feared him because he didn't fit into reality.

I stood and shoved my notebook and pen into my purse, slung it over my shoulder and glanced thankfully at the ocean before I turned my back, stepped into my sandals and walked to my car. I chuckled to myself as I drove, thinking of my exit from the coffee shop without even paying. That poor old man probably thought *I* was the crazy one, flying out of there like the devil himself was after me.

I pulled onto the long, dirt road leading to my house and was relieved to see my cat Cricket dart from the cedar grove to the front steps where he waited for me, doing a little dance step in his impatience. The old boy hadn't come home last night and didn't respond to my call this morning. Although we lived on a narrow country road where traffic wasn't a problem, he had the wanderlust and would take little jaunts for himself. Whenever he didn't show up for breakfast, an extremely important time of day for Cricket, I worried that he'd taken it into his little head to travel over to the main road to hang out and howl with his old cronies. The main road's traffic wasn't merciful to furry creatures.

When I opened the door he dashed in, coming to a halt before his dish with a look of shock and dismay at its emptiness. My other cats, Bess and Jake had taken advantage of his absence and had long since licked the dish clean. I filled it and he noisily smacked his thanks.

My elevated mood gave me energy and the afternoon was spent cleaning my home. I loved my home. I often thought as I came up the long, winding driveway and it suddenly came into view that it looked like a Snow White cottage or a witch's cottage. It snugly fit under the towering oaks and maples and the surrounding shrubs and gardens seemed to protect and nurture it. Although it was an old house it didn't have the traditional small rooms and tiny windows. Whoever had built it knew about light. It was designed so that throughout the day it was flooded with sunlight. It began in the morning with the sun's rays peeping over the meadow and into the kitchen windows. That sunny kitchen was a delight to enter each morning with the yellow light warming it even on the most bitter winter days. As time passed it traveled until it soothed the living room in the late afternoon. Throughout the cottage prisms were hung in every window and the sun's path caused rainbow patches to dance across the walls and floors. Dried herbs hanging in small bunches from the kitchen rafters and spicy candles burning at night permeated the very structure of the house and made one feel they were entering an enchanted place. It *was* an enchanted place. It was magical.

Cricket had found a warm patch of sunlight and was industriously cleaning himself as I watered my jungle of plants. I put a CD on and as I listened to Mozart's music from the soundtrack of *Amadeus,* began to cut vegetables for soup. Such pretty colors and good smells, I thought, as the mixture began to sizzle—red and green peppers, celery, onions, broccoli, cauliflower, shitake mushrooms and scallions. I added beef stock, spices and herbs, covered the pot and left it to slowly simmer.

While the soup was cooking I went into my studio to organize the next week's work. Sitting at my computer table I made a list: create thumbnail sketches for a mural I was to paint in Newton, present a media package for three doctors opening a new practice, finish layouts for a series of newspapers ads, go to the printer on Wednesday, call on a new client on Thursday, order art supplies first thing Monday morning.

Although running an advertising studio brought many problems, caused me to put in long hours and sometimes gave me sleepless nights worrying about money there were definite advantages. I could go into Boston and visit art museums during the day and put my hours in the studio at night. If I completed work for a deadline I could take an afternoon off to go to the ocean with a friend. While my two children were living at home and still in school I was able to be there for them, to take them to piano lessons and to school activities that they would have otherwise missed if I had worked outside the home. Now that they were through college and living on their own it gave me precious time for myself: writing, painting, sculpting, gardening, learning about herbs and their ancient healing properties. There were so many wonderful things to do and to discover I felt I needed several lifetimes to take it all in.

I stopped working when I felt Bess, my matriarch cat, rub against my legs. Bess was a serious and esoteric sort of cat. She worried a great deal and if she were to be thoroughly examined by a scientist I suspect it would be found that she was missing the humor gene. She just didn't get the idea of play and merriment. Even when I plied her with catnip she never indulged in the usual feline gymnastics. She merely stretched out, her head lolling in the saucer that had contained the drugs, her eyes glazed and vacant. Cricket and Jake, on the other hand, were always ready for a good joke or a fast spin around the house, even without benefit of drugs. Yeah, they were the Groucho Marxes of catdom. My main cats.

When I left my studio the soup was ready. That, with a couple of slices of sunflower bread, made a delicious supper while I watched the six o'clock news. I remembered the promise to myself that I wouldn't let it get to me and as each announcement was broadcast I listened objectively, trying to see the overview behind what was happening. I leaned over to the coffee table to pick up my cup and a tingling dizziness came over me as I experienced that same tunnel feeling that I'd had when leaving the ocean.

"Everything is as it should be." The words, reverberating through a corridor from a time before memory, hit me in a rushing torrent like whitewater roaring behind my eyes. The voice was that of the old man in the coffee shop. I wanted to abandon logic and common sense. I wanted to yield to the liquid harmony of his voice.

Oh, God! What was happening to me?

My hands shook as I lifted the cup. Maybe I have a brain tumor. These thoughts and experiences are misfirings in my network. What if there is no old man? What if it's all just the imaginings of a brain being squeezed by a mass of deadly cancer cells?

But what if there *is* an old man who could read my mind, who drew me to him like a magnet, whose smile was like the sun…

What then?

Chapter 2

The Unity

How long must we walk in darkness? Days pass...years, centuries, as pages in a book, leaf after leaf and as each page is turned does it not seem that the truth upon that page is complete? But truth is never complete, always urging us onward, pulling us within its circle, revealing mysteries, dispersing shadows. Can you not feel this deep within you? Have you ever experienced a stirring to ascend, to go beyond, to hold arms out to...something? Yes, it is so intrinsically a part of our being that our entire lives are spent attempting to fulfill the need, the calling.

Step softly with me along the path of these pages, my friends. Approach the threshold of wonder.

After a sleepless night I went to the coffee shop early to beat the after-church crowd. It felt like returning to the scene of the crime. I felt compelled to go back, to see if anyone had noticed the crazy lady running away yesterday, to look for evidence that the old man was real. If he came back, if what I experienced was real? Wouldn't that mean I didn't have a brain tumor? And if I didn't have a tumor what did I have? Hmmmm.

I walked in and headed straight for a booth, trying to look small, to hide in a corner. I glanced around, expecting people to point and whisper, expecting the waitress to say, "Hey, you ripped us off yesterday!" But no one seemed to notice me so, as the waitress brought coffee, I opened my notebook and began writing about my sleepless night during which I watched the digital numbers change on the clock and saw the sky lighten. I had seriously considered that I was going mad. Just another stressed mind gone amok, another statistic of a deteriorating society. The doctor's diagnosis would be, "Ear to ear Jello!" Sometimes after you've had a hard week it doesn't take much to push you over the edge. Someone can innocently say the wrong thing and you burst into tears. I just took this a few (a few!) steps further and walked totally out of reality. You occasionally read about cases like this in the papers. The police find some poor soul with his toe in the electric socket. He left a note: "God told me to do it." Who knows what had happened to make him snap. Life gets to be a bit too much and folks find a way to escape. Robert Frost tells us of the roads we take in life—*Two roads diverged in a wood, and I–I took the one less traveled by…*

    The road my befuddled mind chose to take was way off in left field, a road that was surely "less traveled by," a road that most chose to skirt around, a road that bordered the lunatic fringe and at the end of this road was a mad religious fanatic who had the unique ability to creep into my brain. Joan of Arc heard voices. Don't forget what she experienced as a direct result from straying from the straight and narrow road.

    But, I pondered, if my mind chose to go on a little journey it's best to travel in the company of the godly. I should be thankful that whatever circuitry in my brain was misfiring at least wasn't instructing me to go forth and purchase an automatic weapon. As I was reflecting on the state of my mental health I felt that presence and there was Himself, smiling as if delighted with every little thing and the state of the world. He took off a long, shapeless coat and that odd hat and hung them on a coat rack next to the booth.

"Ahhh, what a beautiful spring morning," he exclaimed, rubbing his hands together. "This morning I watched the marvelous splendor of sunrise. Exquisite, exquisite! Is this universe not a wonder to behold?"

Part of me was relieved that he was there and part was frightened again. He sat down opposite me, folded his hands on the table and began to speak in a low voice, like the whispers of leaves blowing in a forest. "My dear child, do you not know what is happening? Open yourself to that which is within you. Acknowledge Who you are. Begin to live!"

His words melted over me, beginning to thaw the hard suspicious opinion I'd conceived but I fought it, reminding myself of the dangers in today's society. I fought to remember the scam artists who preyed on anyone naive enough to listen to them. I thought of the horror stories told on the TV news about women who trusted strangers but, oh, I wanted to listen to that voice, hear those words. His words spoke of wonders and light and miracles. Oh, Lord, here we go. I'm going to be documented on "Lifestyles of the Thoroughly Demented."

"No, I don't understand. I don't understand anything. You scare the hell out of me!" I moaned. He reached for my hands but I pulled them back, balling them into fists on my lap. "What do you want from me?"

"*From* you?" he asked, "nothing. *For* you...everything."

"That's crazy. You don't even know me," I said defensively.

"Ahhh, but I do." His smile deepened. "From time's beginning I was. From time's beginning you were. We are One. Not one atom of you would pulse with life without me." He closed his eyes. A silence enveloped me like a cocoon of black velvet. The air felt tingly, warm. A glow began to shimmer, not around him or on him but *in* him so that he seemed transparent as if the very atoms that made up his flesh were dancing in joyous movement.

His eyes opened. They contained the universe, radiated an unnamable purity, shimmered in white light, luminous and deep. I floated, sank into them. Within the world of him were stars and moons and suns...galaxies beyond galaxies in perfect harmony, humming, pulsating, reverberating in sound, in music. I knew that all was One and our blue planet, hanging inconceivably in space, pulsated with creative energy. It was bathed in light. It was *alive* and I knew that I, and every living creature, every atom, were part of this throbbing energy, were intertwined, threaded together, interdependent. Every atom within every thing danced in harmony to a vast orchestration. This orchestration was *mind*. This mind was *joy*.

Within his eyes I beheld, on the brink of the infinite, the circle of time. Time was a quantum journey, not linear but a wheel revolving, a vibrating, luminous question. There was no beginning, there was no end. Nothing was born, nothing died. All was in the eternal, boundless wheel. This was unity, our life's search. Ahhhh, let me stay, breathe the timeless. Let me dissolve into it. Let it envelop me like wings, take me in, cover me with love.

My ears roared like thunder as the vision blurred and I was pulled away. Everything within me reached out to hold on to the wonderment. I ached with deep loneliness as I became aware of my body once again. I didn't want to be in it. It felt hard, awkward, alien. I opened my eyes into his. The universe paled, his skin became solid, the glow settled into his depth like stars' light lessening as dawn approached.

I reached out and touched him. "No...no...don't go..."

The eclipse of radiance left me feeling stark, a rocklike mass compressed. I can't live in ordinary life, not after that! I felt the air heavy in my lungs, solid, like trying to inhale ice.

He cupped my chin in his hand, compassion touching my soul, coming from, not just his eyes but from everything in him, circling me like a soft, protective blanket. *"That,"* he whispered, "is what I want for you. I desire that you know your Oneness, that you know the wonder that is life, that your life be a miracle within the miracle."

I inhaled deeply to clear my mind, to make it focus on his words. As I was drawn back to this reality my breathing returned to normal. I forced myself to remain seated as I glanced around me. Everything appeared ordinary: the waitress was wiping the counter, customers were eating and talking, music played.

He answered my unasked question. "They saw nothing. What you experienced was not of the worldly realm." He was patient and allowed me to sit quietly, coming back as if out of a deep sleep. I sipped my coffee and with a shaking hand, set the cup down and sighed heavily. Finally, I was able to speak.

"What is happening to me?" My voice quivered and tears filled my eyes.

He began speaking. I wanted to stay. I wanted to run away. I wanted to go home and hide in bed, sleep and wake up in ordinary reality. I felt ripped from my known world. I have always been searching, sifting through science and spirituality for answers but this...this was like standing over an abyss, fearing to fall into nothingness. This was insanity.

His voice was soft, soothing. "Happening? My dear, you are becoming whole. You have been given a glimpse into *life*! I say that humanity's most intense and joyful moments are but a speck of dust in the universe compared to what is to come."

"Heaven?" I choked out, attempting to distance myself from his magnetic attraction. Surely, he was not about to tell me what I must do to be saved and go to my Great Reward. I'd always found the concept of reward and punishment in the great beyond totally ludicrous.

"I speak not of what humanity, in its limited awareness, has believed. It is not a place, as you know place being an area with boundaries. It is not out there, up there, down there. It is neither a reward nor an experience that must wait until death. It is waiting for you. *It is within you.*"

My eyes widened in incredulity, "Oh, no! No, you're wrong. What I saw was within *you*. All that was in your eyes. How can you say... I can't…"

He held his hand up to stop my protest. "It is within you. Why does that not cause you to celebrate? Why does it frighten you so?"

I gestured in futility. "This is crazy! This is absolute *madness*. I didn't ask for any of this. I didn't ask you to come to me."

"Ahhh, but you did. You called. You searched."

"And that gives you the right to barge in on me...to...to *hypnotize* me? How can you know whether I search or not? Besides, everybody searches, everybody has questions." I rambled on and on in panic, my mind scrambling like a trapped animal, looking for logic, for an escape. Yet another part of my mind, the part that creates, that wonders and imagines was reaching out to him, embracing him, listening entranced.

He waited, allowing me to voice my fears, unperturbed by my anger, my diatribe. I sat, finally silent, staring out the window at the budding trees and the traffic along the road. When I glanced at him he was looking at me with question in his eyes. "Do you know Who I am?"

"I don't know anything," I answered despondently. I felt beaten.

"That is the beginning of all-knowing. It is first to empty oneself of all preconceptions. Then one is standing naked, ready to receive truth."

"And what is that?" I asked, my throat tightening, asking the question that had been asked for eons—"What is truth?"

"Go into the forest and there you will learn truth. Embrace the wind and she will whisper truth. Befriend the night. Listen."

I heard his cryptic answer but felt only exhaustion. Never have I been so depleted, so numb. The waitress came over to the table, filled my cup and left without even acknowledging the man across from me. Oh, my god, perhaps he wasn't there!

"I have left you much to ponder. Meditate and I will give you comfort."

And he was gone. I mean...*gone*. He didn't walk out. He vanished!

This time I didn't run from the coffee shop. I just sat there dazed, drinking my coffee and staring out the window. Tears welled up in my eyes as I experienced a bittersweet feeling of longing. I looked down at my notebook and there, scrawled across the page in a bold, masculine handwriting were the words:

"I give you my comfort."

René Donovan

Chapter 3

The Dawning

*Nothing will usher in peace but a full spiritual awakening.
As you approach the spiritual you must put aside all fixed
concepts. There is no distinct line between the seen and the
unseen. It is a merging. Our bondage to the past is at it
twilight. The wondermnent of the future is at its dawn.
Know that the time between dusk and dawn
is a time of deep changes.
Do we dare speak of these changes?
Do we dare not*

To say that my life changed that day would be an understatement. It brought me up short, like hitting a stone wall. I'd been walking a long, bumpy path and was suddenly thrust onto another, one leading away from everything known. Before I had left the coffee shop I called the waitress over and asked her to tell me what was written on that page in my notebook. I couldn't believe my own eyes. Perhaps I could believe hers. She turned to better see it, read aloud, "I give you my comfort," frowned then looked at me, puzzled. I thanked her and she left, shaking her head. She probably thought I was one of those religious nuts who walk around handing out business cards that read, "Jesus loves you." Jeez, she didn't know the half of it. I don't simply have deep religious convictions. Do I dare even think this? *I believe I've met God.*

I sat there pondering this: If I really was crazy this wouldn't bother me, would it? I mean, I would be *convinced*. People who suffer delusion don't question their own hallucinations. If they think they're Jesus Himself they would just go ahead and surround themselves with all the props: the robe, sandals, hairstyle, even find a cross. Then they'd commence to roam about preaching, being wise and forgiving or whatever they perceive Jesus to have been. They wouldn't think twice about this stuff. Conviction doesn't question.

After my traumatic Sunday morning visit from Whoever I canceled all business appointments and spent a week in solitude, time which was filled with his words chanting in my mind like a mantra, "I give you my comfort." Some comfort. I was seriously considering calling my doctor to schedule an MRI exam just to take a little peek to see what's happening. Did this comfort include screening my phone calls, not talking to my children or friends? I couldn't pretend nothing was wrong. I wasn't sleeping at night because I kept hearing his voice. Maybe he's some kind of conjurer, a magician like David Copperfield, I thought. I once saw him make the Statue of Liberty disappear. Maybe this was the result of too much caffeine. Will there soon be an announcement—"The Surgeon General has determined that consuming large quantities of caffeine results in mental confusion and hallucinations."

I felt caught between two worlds. Everything seemed important. Nothing seemed important. I began reading everything in my bookshelves on religion or spirituality. I went to the library and checked out stacks of books on abnormal psychology, brain tumors, cult leaders. Each day I awoke, after a few restless hours of sleep, packed a lunch and left the house. I walked long, sandy stretches by the ocean, wandered deep into the woods where I sat under trees writing, reading and listening to music under headphones: Vivaldi, Chopin, Mozart, Mahler. The sounds of their genius followed me through the hours, the days. I began reading the New Testament, something I hadn't done since childhood when the words were meaningless. Biographies of Walt Whitman stunned me. He could easily be the man in the coffee shop. The photographs of Whitman were identical to the old man in the coffee shop, right down to that wide-brimmed hat. Passages from Emerson, Thoreau, William Blake, Buddha, Behmen, Tennyson, Wordsworth and others spoke of enlightenment, of seeing the light, of experiencing a new consciousness.

Could this be it? Could I be experiencing *enlightenment*? No, not possible. I mean, this didn't happen to ordinary people like me. Did it?

Was Whitman an ordinary person until he knew that *something* which impelled him to write, "I cannot be awake, for nothing looks to me as it did before, or else I am awake for the first time, and all before has been a mean sleep."

Was Longfellow typical of others until enlightenment gave him these words:

> *So comes to us at times, from the unknown*
> *And inaccessible solitudes of being,*
> *The rushing of the sea-tides of the soul:*
> *And inspirations that we deem our own*
> *Are some divine foreshadowing and foreseeing*
> *Of things beyond our reason or control.*

Of things beyond our reason or control. This surely was what I was experiencing. This element ran through so many of the great minds—that there is something to attain that is far beyond the ordinary human life. But...no....not for me. I was sitting in a *coffee shop*, of all places, writing about such ordinary fears, nothing lofty or spiritual.

The eighth day of solitude dawned with darkened skies and a driving rain. My retreat from society ended when I realized the refrigerator and cupboards were almost empty. One can of cat food left! A dangerous situation, indeed. The thought of being alone in the house with three hungry cats was scary. I cleaned the house, changing the sheets on my bed, doing two washes and answering some of my phone messages and then left the house. Hours later, after grocery shopping, going to the recycling station, returning books to the library and other errands, I returned home. The cats were fed (whew!) and groceries were put away. I made a fire in the wood stove and lay on the couch for a quick nap.

It was dark when I awoke, the house silent except for the rain hitting the windows and the wind whistling down the chimney. The fire was out and the house was cold. After turning on the light by my head, I sat up and rubbed my face, trying to push away the grogginess. I stumbled into the kitchen where the clock read 7:45 and decided that I was too tired to cook and would go to the coffee shop for supper. I'd take one of my books and read while I enjoyed one of their house specialties. Of course, I wasn't about to admit to myself there might be another reason for going there. A week had passed since my last encounter with...Whatever...and I suspect I just wanted to sort of test the waters. Maybe God would pop in and buy me a sandwich. Tee hee.

Oh, God, I groaned, I'm *nuts*.

The roads were empty as I drove, the wind battered the car, pulled leaves from the trees and pasted them against the windshield. What am I doing out here, I thought? I considered returning home, cooking up some pasta and calling it a night but decided that since I was almost there I'd just keep going. A few minutes later I pulled into the parking lot.

It looked warm and inviting inside where a few people sat drinking coffee, hunched over newspapers. The red and white checked curtains and knotty pine walls gave a New England essence which was heightened by the always present aromas of home cooking. I always enjoyed coming here, alone or with friends and long, intimate conversations over cup after cup of coffee. Every small New England town has these coffee shops where locals go every morning, the favorite spot where you always find someone to chat with. But it's not everyone's good fortune to meet Walt Whitman or even—God. (Won't be long now. I'll be untroubled on a nice Thorazine vacation.)

I stepped from the car and pulled my coat collar around my face, trying to hide from the cold rain. As I walked the few steps to the front door I heard the terrible sound, like the wailing of a prehistoric animal. The seemingly endless squeal of brakes ended with the explosion of impact.

The accident happened at the traffic lights about fifty feet away. A pickup truck had collided with a small foreign car, pushing it onto the sidewalk, folded like a toy. The ensuing silence was eerie. The men from the coffee shop pushed through the door, almost knocking me to the ground. I leaned against the building to regain my footing, then took a few steps forward, feeling I should be trying to help. That's when I felt someone grip my arm and turned to see the old man standing next to me.

"The damn door's jammed!" one of the men yelled as he banged on the door with his fist then ran around to the passenger side where he found the door locked. He began pounding on the windows. Another voice said, "There's a little girl in there too! Oh, God, no! I think they're both dead."

The three men were joined by the driver of the truck, who appeared unhurt. "She came out of nowhere! I couldn't stop! Oh, please...let them be all right," he cried.

One of the men held him back. "Don't look. Make sure somebody's called the police." He gave the man a little shove toward the coffee shop. "Go ahead."

I looked up at the old man, our eyes met and I silently pleaded with him. Whoever he was I knew he could help. His eyes seemed to bleed with pity, the screams of eternity lay within their depths. He turned from me, rain pouring from his hat, his stride purposeful as he approached the scene. The other men fell silent and stepped aside as the old man, with that quiet authority, placed both hands on the car's roof. The door seemed to melt and then swung open.

They stared, dumbfounded. One of them muttered, "I'll be damned."

The old man leaned into the car and placed his fingers on the woman's forehead. She stirred and raised her head, dazed. Then he gently lifted the child and cradled her against his massive chest. The scene was surreal: the black night, the howling wind, torrential rain and the growl of thunder in the distance...and everyone surrounding the old man who knelt on the pavement, the child within the circle of his arms. He threw back his head, eyes skyward, and cried, "I weep for my children!" It seemed that the entire universe, all of creation, all love wailed those words. The words were spoken and now everything must change. The words echoed through the past, into the future. They reverberated, they were electric.

Then the night was hushed. He bent down and kissed the little girl between her eyebrows, the same tender spot that he had touched on the mother. The child's wounds that had caused death began to close and fade. Blood that had covered both mother and child disintegrated. The little girl stirred. Her eyes opened and she gazed up at the old man then wrapped her arms around his neck. As she lay curled against his chest he rocked her, murmuring soothing words in her ear. She nodded, a transcendent smile upon her tiny mouth.

When the mother realized her daughter was not dead, only then were tears released. She sobbed heavily and held her arms out. The old man handed the child to her and was heard to say, "The child is whole."

The shriek of sirens drew our attention and soon the area was flashing with red and blue lights blurring all into a landscape of confusion. Policemen were questioning everyone as the ambulance attendants sped off with their two passengers. The man who'd been driving the truck was taken to the police station. I walked slowly into the coffee shop as the tow truck, chains rattling, hooked the rear of the wrecked car. The waitress, Shelly, was standing by the door and asked, "Was anyone hurt? I saw them put people in the ambulance."

I shook my head and lowered myself onto a stool, leaning on the counter for support. She brought a cup of coffee and said in a motherly way, "Are you okay? Why don't you take off that wet coat? Here," she reached under the counter and handed me a towel, "Go into the ladies' room and dry your hair. Goodness, you're going to catch your death o' cold."

She seemed to be in her element as she fussed and mothered. Then she turned her attention to the men as they walked through the door, shaking caps and hanging up coats. When I returned from the washroom, Shelly had everyone settled with steaming cups of coffee and nurturing advice. Everyone seemed to be avoiding what really took place out there, not ten minutes ago.

The men seemed to know each other and were talking in good-natured relief that no one, after all, had been hurt. They discussed the whys, hows and wherefores of the accident but no one mentioned that the mother and her child had been *dead*. Not one person, including myself, dared to voice what everyone had to be thinking—*what, in God's name, happened out there?*

Every head turned as the old man walked through the door. The silence was potent as the communal breath was held. He sat with us but seemed apart, deep in thought. Finally, one of the men, leaning his elbows on the counter and looking past the man seated beside him, addressed the old man. "So, what do you think about...all that?" He jerked his thumb in the direction of the parking lot.

A slight smile curved the corners of the old man's mouth. He raised his eyebrows in question and asked, "Tell me, Robert, what have *you* to say about it?"

Robert, a throwback to the 60s with long, graying hair pulled back into a braid and sporting granny glasses, grinned nervously. He glanced at the other men, shook his head and answered, "Damnedest thing I ever saw. When I looked in that car," he rubbed his face as if trying to erase the image in his mind, "I thought they were both dead but then..." he shrugged, "I don't know. I don't know what the hell went on out there." In his confusion Robert didn't notice that the old man knew his name.

The old man nodded. "It did seem that was the way of it." All eyes were on him, waiting for an explanation, something they could understand. He continued, "There is no death."

The men looked at each other, puzzled, and their voices buzzed down the line of seats. "What did he say?" asked Jeff, a tall black man.

"There's no death," Robert muttered, scowling.

"Oh, cut the bull! I saw what I saw," Jeff angrily argued. "*They were dead.* I was in Nam and I know dead when I see it."

The old man held up his hands and the words he spoke sent shivers down my spine. "What you have witnessed tonight is the beginning."

The silence that followed lasted a full minute. Shelly stopped wiping the counter and stood, nervously clutching the towel. As if in a stage setting and on cue to heighten the drama, thunder rumbled.

Don, a tall, thin man wearing boots, jeans and plaid wool jacket, ran his fingers through thick, blond hair, cleared his throat and asked, "Beginning...beginning of what?" He seemed frightened by the answer to come.

How is he going to answer that question? Will he tell us who he is, where he came from? Will he show them what he showed to me? I barely believed it myself. Shelly quietly left her post behind the counter and sat on the vacant stool to my right. She nudged me and whispered, "What did he do?"

What could I say to her? He brought two people back from the dead? Instead, I said, "You wouldn't believe..."

He began speaking. "The time is come to leave the darkness. Now is the beginning of the Age of Spirit."

Jeff, the man who had been in Vietnam, spoke up, "I don't understand." Then with anger in his voice he asked, "Who *are* you?"

"You may call me Walt." He glanced at me and winked. He knew. He knew that I felt he looked like Whitman. Thoughts came to me as if they were placed in my head from him: he came as one we would accept, he came as a benevolent figure. In order for us to listen he took on human form.

The others accepted his answer that his name was Walt but their other questions were still unanswered. Jeff regarded him warily and said, "But that doesn't tell us what you did out there or what this stuff is about this...this age of spirit."

"Have you not seen the signs? You have been living in the Age of Reason, the limitation of the five senses. It has been a masculine world, violent, unbalanced. The results of this are pouring forth upon you now and my people are empty, confused and frightened. This is pushing you to reach out for the new path of the spirit."

Robert pushed his glasses up on his nose and rubbed the stubble on his chin. "What's going on here, Walt? Some thoughts are going through my head. I don't want to say what. Don't speak fancy words. Just come right out and tell us what you have to say."

Walt smiled almost sadly as he turned his full attention to Robert. "When I tell you, Robert, will you believe?"

"Try me. Then I'll tell you if I believe you," he answered softly and sincerely.

Walt rose from where he had been sitting and slowly walked along the curve of the counter. "*I am.*"

As these words were spoken a radiance filled him, a warmth of love emanated from him and encircled the group seated at the counter. The lights overhead dimmed as his glow increased. All eyes shone, as if by firelight, transfixed, taking in his love as ones who are thirsty. Tears streamed down my cheeks as I felt the wonder of him. My long week of solitude and retreat, the doubts and fears waned as I shared this experience with others.

The glow began to fade and there was a brief moment of darkness until the overhead lights flickered, then caught. No one moved. Not a sound was heard until ripping sobs escaped from Jeff.

Walt's deep, compassionate voice continued, "I will answer the questions that are in your hearts. I am with you. I have always been with you, closer that your very breath. I have loved and spoken to all my beloved people but you heard not, you saw not for the world was so heavily upon you. Long ago it was told to you, "The kingdom of heaven is within. *I* am within you, your very self."

As we were digesting his words he sat once again with us. "I have come in the form of a most elevated man—Walt Whitman. Ahhh, my Whitman. While on his earth's journey he lived as few other. He knew! He had evolved beyond the ordinary and truly saw *life* and like others before him, wanted only to give this gift of spirit to others. He once wrote, '...for I bestow upon any man or woman the entrance to all the gifts of the universe.' He knew the secret of truly entering spirit. For, you see, he enjoyed *everything* in his life. There was no separation of spirit and matter.

"Many people seeking a spiritual life feel that they must conquer the body's senses, live in poverty and find no joy in this wondrous gift called life but, oh, my Whitman," he sighed. "He lived his life fully as it was meant to be lived, in delight, savoring every day. Through time and beyond time there have been others…"

He stood and there before us was transformed. A shimmering glow touched him and his wondrous face became that of an ancient Native American woman. Her face was deeply, darkly wrinkled and wisdom shone from her sparkling black eyes. She was tiny, about five feet tall but seemed to hold a dignified power within her. Long gray braids fell over her shoulders and were wound with beaded rawhide. She wore what one would imagine a woman of her culture and time would wear: a dark, soft leather tunic over wide-legged pants and beaded moccasins on her feet. She smiled and told us her name was "Grandmother."

As we watched, Grandmother faded and a strong, black face took her place. A proud face. She was clearly a woman of authority. She merely smiled at us and began to merge with another presence. An Asian man stood before us in a white robe, acknowledging us with a slight bow before transforming into a tall woman in black robes. Between her eyebrows was a blue mark, a sort of tattoo. Upon her long black hair she wore a headdress of two silver half-moons on either side of a full moon. She held her arms high, the sleeves of her robes falling down her arms, and began to chant. Her voice was otherworldly and seemed to be many voices in unison, words I couldn't understand but words that called out to me. I closed my eyes and swayed to the ethereal rhythm and it felt as if her voice were drumming, drumming. I was enchanted. A feeling entered me: I have done this before, long years before. I have stood within a circle, danced, celebrated Mother Earth and have been enraptured.

The chanting faded and I opened my eyes. The old poet stood before us. Smiling, he held out his hands and said, "So, you see, my friends. I am All. I am woman, I am man, I am all nations, all colors, all races, all faiths." He lay his big hands upon the countertop and whispered, "*I Am.*"

Lines from Whitman's poem *Song of Myself* came to me: "To be in any form, what is that?"

What held us here? Shouldn't a situation like this cause people to panic, to run away? How is it that we can stay here and talk with him, ask questions, not erupt in an explosion of insanity? My mind wanted to fit this neatly into a known experience, to label it.

Jeff's voice, hoarse with tears and emotion, was heard, "Can I ask...can I ask...why? Why us?"

Walt sighed deeply, touched his forehead, deep in thought, then began, "See yourselves not at *chosen,* as ones singled out as superior to others. I am entering the open minds, the humble minds, those that are truly searching." He glanced around the counter to include everyone. "This new path you will travel will be in your hearts, an individual experience but flowing from one to another."

Robert cleared his throat and caught Walt's attention. "Are you asking us to start a new *church?*" His voice clearly indicated that this was a reprehensible request.

Walt shook his head emphatically, "Too often the formation of a church results in separation. What I speak of is an *evolution.*"

"Evolution to what?"

Walt's arms extended as if to take in the entire universe. "To peace. For only when your hearts have lifted beyond the insecurity that is like a disease today will your planet experience peace. Real peace is not an absence of war. It is a fullness within each individual, a fullness that knows no insecurity."

Don removed his jacket, flipped his hair out of his eyes, sipped his coffee and said, Walt, you still haven't said what you want of us."

"I appear to many people, as many people and this has been ongoing for eons but now people all over this planet are experiencing what you are experiencing. A seed is being planted and amazing changes have begun. The balancing of the male and female energies will begin to inspire security and human beings will evolve to become as wise as Whitman, as Jesus, as the Buddha. For indeed, this is what these inspired beings tried to teach you. They did not intend to be founders of religion but to be teachers of men and women, to inspirit them to evolve beyond their petty selves. I have come to show you Who you truly are."

Shelly tentatively touched Walt's arm and asked in a soft voice, "Are you the second coming?"

He tilted his head, ran his fingers through his gray beard and answered, "How can spirit come again when spirit has never left you?"

Her curly brown hair framed a face of pure innocence, despite her middle years. Wide blue eyes were upon Walt as if she about to fall on her knees. "How do we...I mean, if you are..."

Walt knew her thoughts. "My dear child, how do you wish that others relate to *you*? Would you feel at one with those who were bowed down before you, mumbling of their unworthiness? I ask no one to bow. Would you ask that your children grovel at your feet? Would you find joy in their debasement? As a child, could you truly love a parent who demanded such behavior of you? Do you fall down with your face to the ground before a sunset? No, you become filled with it, you feel communion. You are not separate from me. This has always been so, since your birth, since the birth of time itself." He reached out for her and she leaned against him and as she did so I could see a change come across her face, a look of delighted surprise. I knew that feeling. You feel as if you've come home.

He patted her back in a fatherly way. She remained with him for a few moments and when she returned to the seat beside me there was a definite change in her, a transformation in her eyes. Where before she seemed almost timid, gazing at him in adoration, now she appeared somehow stronger within a deep in delight. Have I, too, undergone such an alteration? I felt drawn to him, felt love for him but, unlike the time I got lost in his eyes it wasn't idolatry, a readiness to lose myself in him. He gave something. I suddenly realized that he gave me *myself.*

"If you knew Who you truly are you would be incapable of fear, doubt, anger, jealousy or deceit." He sat down and reached for the cup of coffee Shelly had poured for him earlier, drank from the cup and sighed contentedly, as if it were elixir. "Your potential is limitless. Your wonder-fullness and goodness are boundless. You are loved beyond any love you now know. Can you begin to believe that all your fears are illusions? Can you see that you do not stop where your skin ends? You are not separate from your brothers and sisters or from the stars or oceans, or trees, or rabbits, or cows...or from the Source of creation."

When his words ended the silence was heavy. The words were said with such gentleness and love yet with such power that they seemed to hang in the very air we breathed. How, I wondered, is it that we can sit in this ordinary place, in this ordinary time and speak with this remarkable man? How is it that we can converse so sanely in the midst of the hushed center of the earth? I toyed with my spoon, making coffee-patterns on the table. Is it possible to live without fear, doubt, deceit? How can it be that they are illusions?

He answered my thoughts when he turned toward me and said,

"Science is showing you the illusion. If you would but study the discoveries of your scientists you would see that for centuries they have been sifting through matter to find pure energy. Quantum physics breaks down matter and, like a Chinese puzzle, each segment discovered broken down to yet a smaller segment: matter into atoms, molecules, protons, neutrons, quarks. As each 'layer' is pealed back to reveal the energy within they come closer to the pure energy of life. All that exists is made up of one energy, vibrating at various rates, creating degrees of density. Matter breaks down to energy, energy into light." He held his hands cupped together, then opened them as if releasing the secret. "This energy and light is *malleable by mind.*" He paused, searching our faces. "Is this not truly miraculous?"

"The energy is the music and dance of the universe. My Einstein knew the song of creation. He once wrote, 'To know that what is impenetrable to us really exists, manifesting itself as the highest wisdom and the most radiant beauty, which our dull facilities can comprehend only in the most primitive forms...this knowledge, this feeling is at the center of true religiousness. In this sense, and in this sense only, I belong to the ranks of the devoutly religious men.'"

To be with him, to hear him speak was not what one would imagine. He inspired, not dumbstruck adoration, but love, deep friendship, kinship. Had hours passed, minutes, days? I had no concept of time while in his company. It was still dark outside, the rain still fell in windblown sheets rattling the windows. I heard his voice, that deep melodious voice rumbling along with the thunder in the sky.

And then all was gone. I was home, lying on the couch in the darkness, the wind whistling down the chimney, cats curled up all around me but that voice, that rumbling thunder-voice spoke to me: "Is this not truly miraculous?" Somehow...nothing else mattered.

René Donovan

Chapter 4

The Balance

Does it not seem that we in our evolution have reached a wall? Yes, and now we must see the crack in the wall, place our hands within it and open the hardness which has kept us imprisoned. Our path has been a horizontal one with many detours. In cracking through the wall our path will become vertical, on a silver thread through creation to form a pattern with the Light. Within this pattern you will witness the male and the female, the two sides of creation, the double thread.

This, my friends, weaves the totality of life.

"It is beginning, beginning..." The words rang through me and separated me from my dream state. I awoke with a start, heart pounding. I lay back on the pillow with a relieved sigh, wondering what, in those words, had frightened me. If anything, they were reassuring. My mind stilled and tried to grasp the dream fragments. It was dark. There was anger. It was ominous. Someone...who...someone was after me, threatening me. I was walking down a grassy path between two boulders, huge gray-black mountainous rocks looming on either side of me. I was afraid to walk between them but someone was calling me. As I neared the end of this rock corridor the Native woman that I had seen in last night's vision stepped onto the path. The moon's light pooled upon her. In her hands she held an urn, about two feet tall. She held it out to me and said, "When this be filled with your tears then you enter the kingdom of heaven."

"But, Grandmother," I pleaded, "what about laughter?"

Grandmother looked at me, those luminous black eyes reaching deep, "Laughter can not be contained."

I received the urn from her and turned to leave and saw what had frightened me. Behind me, up on a hill in the darkness was a man. It was not his appearance that caused such dread for he looked quite ordinary. It was what emanated from him—malevolence. He merely stood and watched me but the loathing seemed to ooze around him like a second hideous skin.

That was when I awoke. Oh, great, I thought. I'm looking for something new to worry about. After all I'd seen why wasn't I flowing in a peaceful stream of certainty? My son Mark called it my "worry space." He said that when I had a big problem it filled my worry space and when that problem was solved, I gathered little worries to fill it. I don't believe my worry space has ever been empty.

Here I was, having meetings with the Top Brass for heaven's sake, even got myself a peek into the cosmos. Why was I still poking about trying to find some life-trash? Habit, I guess. The fear habit is hard to break. When things begin to go well I get a little nervous. "Oops, can't let down the ole' guard!" While I'm smiling like a fool no telling what sort of foul thing might come sneaking up on me and lay its bony, toady fingers on the back of my neck. I could almost see Walt shaking a finger and admonishing me, "Oh, ye of little faith."

Oh, Walt, I'm trying. It's not easy—being human. I wondered what Shelly and the men were thinking about this morning. What about that mother and her little girl? Even though I had found myself lying on the couch last night with no memory of having left the coffee shop and driven home it was so *real*. The experience was more profound than was reason. Was I just wanting to believe it had happened because the alternative, that my mind was hanging on by a rusty thread, flapping about with any chill breeze that came along, was too unbearable?

I groaned and pulled myself from bed. I should make some calls and set up some appointments, do some work in the studio. I should mow the lawn, clean the car, find out what that funny smell was in the refrigerator but I could not force myself to settle down into work. My mind was flying, soaring in the macrocosm. I kept thinking of the dream. "When this is filled with your tears…" Hmmm. I've probably shed enough tears in my lifetime to fill many of Grandmother's urns. I could overflow an Olympic-size swimming pool!

While the coffee was brewing I cut fruit for breakfast and thought about the angel appearing to Mary, telling her a bit of rather startling news. According to the story she was confused but gracefully accepted. How could she do that? I mean, she not only had a chat with an angel, which is pretty unconventional, but she had to tell her betrothed that she'd gotten pregnant in a very bizarre manner. "Listen, Joe. I've got something to tell you. You're just not going to *believe* this! (giggle, giggle) Now, promise you won't get mad but…" Whew! At least I didn't have *that* to contend with. Walt must know my limitations. All I'd need right now is to see three camels strolling up my driveway.

I showered, dressed, filled my backpack with books, notebook, pens, cassette player and tapes, left the house and headed…yes, to the coffee shop. No, I didn't want another little tryst. I wanted to sit peacefully over a cuppa' and write in my notebook about last night's adventure, or whatever it was, and this morning's dream.

Inside the coffee shop I glanced around. Coast clear? As usual, everything appeared normal so I settled in at an empty booth, opened my notebook and began writing. Not two minutes into it I felt a hand on my shoulder. Startled, expecting to see my Pal, I looked up. Shelly's eyes met mine.

"Would you like some company?" she asked nervously.

"That would be great!" I answered, moving my books and notebook. She sat opposite me and signaled to the waitress to bring coffee.

"I'm not working today but I had a feeling you'd be here. I have to talk with you."

I nodded grimly. "You think you're going crazy?"

"Oh, God, yes! *What* is going on? I found myself sitting here all by myself last night. One minute I was…" she lowered her voice, "with you and those men and….and…"

"Walt?" I finished for her.

We were silent as the waitress set two cups of coffee on the table and asked, "Anything else?"

I shook my head and Shelly answered the waitress. "Thanks, Judy. No, coffee's all."

Sighing, I stirred sugar and cream in the cup and said, "I'm glad you came. I needed someone to talk to about all this."

She groaned and muttered, "Yeah, it's not exactly something you take to your mother." She grasped the edge of the table and hissed between clenched teeth, "What-the-hell-is-happening?"

I smiled at her theatrics but had no words of comfort or explanation. I felt we had entered a carnival funhouse where up was down and anything could lie just beyond the next corner. "It feels like madness," I admitted, "but now at least if I'm crazy I have company. Before last night I was all alone in this and…"

She gasped and leaned closer toward me. "It happened to you before last night?"

I sipped my coffee and nodded. "Twice."

"No! Twice? What happened?" she asked, her eyes widening in amazement.

I told her about the previous encounters with Walt, the feelings of him talking in my head and the dream. We shared our experience of last night. Finally, I asked, "Do you have anything planned for today?"

She shook her head, "I canceled everything. I'm just going to hang out and...think, I guess."

"Want to hang out and think with me?" I asked. "I was going to go to the ocean, do some reading, some writing." I showed her my notebook and told her all I had been writing.

We drove in my car the fifteen minutes to the ocean, this time to a place called, "The Cliffs," an estate of about fifty acres, which had been owned by an old, prestigious New England family for generations. Two roads ran through it, one up a hill where there were four houses, the other ran along the ocean side high above the water. This road ended at a little house with a wraparound porch. This was my favorite house at the Cliffs and I've often fantasized that it was my home and in the morning I could walk out onto the porch and greet the morning sun by my beloved ocean. All the houses were old with weathered shingles but the other four were huge, gothic structures, somewhat intimidating. *My* little cottage was friendly and inviting.

As we walked up the narrow road Shelly asked, "No one minds if you come here?"

"No one lives here except in the summer," I answered, my eyes following the flight of sparrows. "The caretaker never says anything except to the kids who come here to party."

"It's so beautiful," she sighed. "So peaceful."

"I come here sometimes when I have to think. My favorite time was one morning after a big snowstorm. I got up while it was still dark and came here with my camera and a thermos of coffee. The wind had curled the snow into frozen peaks like dairy-queen ice cream. When the sun came up it turned them pink, orchid, red. It was glorious! I got some exceptional photos. I'll show them to you sometime."

We were developing a friendship. I felt connected to her. We had shared something extraordinary, to say the least, and that had created a bond. She was a few years younger than I. Her hair showed a few strands of white whereas mine was streaked, white wings at my temples combining with the black. She dressed as I did in sneakers, jeans, sweater but was full-figured, unlike me who had always been slim. Like all new friends, we were curious about each others' lives. She had two teenage boys, both away in college. Divorced and since she seemed sensitive to that hurt, I didn't question further. While studying to be a massage therapist she worked two jobs: one was waitressing in the coffee shop at night, the other was creating pottery in her home and selling her work in shops and craft shows all over New England.

We walked in comfortable silence for a while, enjoying the spring day, the fields of grass now greening under the sun's warmth, the sound of the surf hissing on the beach below. Then she turned to me and confided, "Diana, I'm scared of all this, afraid of what it means. There's something in the future that I don't think I want."

"But what can we do?" I asked. "We haven't exactly volunteer for any of this. It *happened* to us."

"I'm not so sure about that," she said. "Walt told us that he came to minds that were searching. From what you've told me about yourself you've been looking for answers all your life. Since I can remember I've been different from others. I was overweight as a child and unless you live that you can never understand the torture from other kids. So I became a loner and when other girls were having slumber parties then dating boys I was in the library, walking alone in the woods, painting, writing poetry. The good thing about being different is that you learn to love solitude."

I stopped to pick up a beautifully shaded round stone and said, "I lived in the country, the youngest of three girls. My sisters were six and eight years older than I and there were no other children around so I learned to love my own company. I enjoyed the same things you did, walking in the woods, painting, writing. When I was little I used to lie on the ground in the woods and stay really still so that I could see fairies."

She laughed. "Did you ever spot one?"

"Only in my imagination. I still have a wild imagination. When all this began happening to me I thought that my fantasies had just taken me way out of reality."

We both heard the music at the same time and stopped to listen. Someone was playing a flute and the melody was carried to us on the sea-wind, a haunting, chanting kind of sound. Then we saw someone at the far end of the field and from the way she held her body we knew this was the flutist. Hesitantly, we walked toward the sound.

The woman turned, as we approached, lowered the instrument from her mouth and smiled. Shelly grasped my hand and whispered, "Oh, my God!"

We stood near her, staring transfixed, dumbstruck. It was Grandmother. She turned her face and gazed out to sea, a sadness over her features. "I come as Walt comes," she said simply. Her voice was surprisingly clear and strong for someone so tiny and so old.

Good god, what is this! I wondered in alarm. Am I living the story of Scrooge, being visited by three spirits? Will Jacob Marley come clanking into the coffee shop one day, hefting his chains, whisking me off for a preview of my tombstone? Come Christmas morning will I go racing through the streets and, in a manic outburst, hand out turkeys to amend my sins?

She chuckled silently, her shoulders shaking. "Walt say you make him laugh, you be so funny." She tucked her flute into a leather case tied to her waist, took our hands and began leading us through the field, down an incline and onto the beach.

We walked, hand in hand. Sometimes, I guess, you just can't question. After Walt, after last night I'd believe anything. If a genie appeared in my bedroom and ate my mattress I'd take it in stride. "Yup, I believe. Fairies, wee folk, Santa, little gray men...show them the way to my house. I'll let them in, feed them, be best friends. Uh huh."

I heard a chuckle from Grandmother. "You not believe *everything*!" she said.

My mind was right on the edge. It wouldn't take much now. Teetering on the precipice...a teensy shove...*there I go!* I'll wander forever in the land of Odd, I'll....

"Oh, you not crazy. Don't you be worrying about that," she gently scolded, her dark eyes sparkling with mischief.

Oh, sure. Easy for her to say. She's not the one who's walked through the Thorazine Doorway. I glanced at her and frowned when I saw her shaking with suppressed laughter.

"You listen now to Grandmother," she advised as we walked, "and you learn many things. You pay attention 'cause you going to need wisdom in days to come. People have to listen to old ways or they're not going to have a safe home any more."

Shelly and I glanced at each other over Grandmother's head. Shelly raised her eyebrows and shrugged her shoulders as if to say, "Whatever..."

Despite her size Grandmother strode along at a fast pace until we came to a spot where a willow tree overhung the water. She wore a woven shawl around her shoulders and pulled the ends across her chest as a gust of wind came off the ocean. Then she nimbly sat in the sand, legs crossed and patted the place beside her, indicating that we should join her.

We both instinctively knew that it was not time to ask questions, that she was here for a reason that we would soon know. She withdrew her flute from its case and began playing again, a different tune this time, a tune from long ago, a Native song. Her breath made the flute come alive as long, sad notes rolled around us. It made me feel melancholy like it was telling a sorrowful story. The scent of sea salt was heavy in the air as if rising to greet this ancient being.

When the last note sighed she lay the flute on her lap and began. "Walt, Grandmother, Great Spirit, all the same. Long time ago my spirit lived an earth-life as a woman of great power in my tribe. I had visions when I was a little child. I saw the future of my tribe, of all Native people. I saw white-skinned people come to our lands. I saw them multiply like snowflakes piling up in great storm. I saw what would happen to the land all over the planet. I heard the wailing of the spirits of my people. I took my visions to the elders and they wondered at such things. 'Could this be?' they would ask each other. After first visions I had many, many more. I traveled through time, saw things, knew things. I could heal all sick ones of my tribe. When the time came for ceremony to enter lodge of women I was named Spirit Woman because I traveled between worlds. As years came upon me and I was an elder I was called Grandmother because I was like Grandmother to many, many people. When I left that life I was told of the years to come and of great destruction these strange people would unleash upon earth. I was told that one day my spirit would come back to help heal Mother Earth. I would come back and blend with others' spirits." She paused, her eyes seeming to gaze at something far away.

"So," she resumed haltingly, "in spirit I knew it be time, time for female energy to rise up, to touch people, to fill hearts. Mother Earth had been too long in male energy. All male energy causing problems you see now."

"Grandmother!" Shelly interrupted. "You can't be saying that all men are bad!"

Grandmother drew back her head and scowled. "You hear me say that? I speak of *energy!* Men have one kind of energy, women have another. When only one energy running things everything get unbalanced. If all women energy be running things that would cause big mess too!

"I bring earth-wisdom. I bring female-wisdom." She wound her fingers together to represent joining and said, "Every thread in creation be woven together but thread of humans unraveling whole pattern."

I thought of a TV documentary in which a huge area of a national park was in ruins. Everything was dying, from the wetlands, to the grasses and the fish and animals. Ecologists studied the situation and came to the conclusion that the area was being destroyed because the wolves had been obliterated. Over time this caused a chain reaction through Nature, which is so carefully and precisely balanced.

I gazed out to sea, not wanting to meet Grandmother's eyes. What humans have done in their ignorance and arrogance. Not just other people but myself as well: the waste, the hurt unintentionally inflicted. Finally I met Grandmother's eyes and admitted, "Sometimes I feel so guilty for all the stupid things I've done in my life."

"You do something bad Grandmother not know about?" she asked, leaning close and turning my face toward her so that our eyes met.

"Oh, you know what I mean. I've messed up so much. When I look back on…"

Grandmother took my hand and asked in a firm voice, "Why you mess up, hmmm? Why you make mistakes, do foolish things?"

She listened patiently while I stumbled over excuses: "I never meant to. I never…"

She grasped my hand tightly and said, "It be because you not know any better at that time. You be in stage of life when you just not know how to do different. That be right?" I nodded in agreement and she asked another question. "You wiser now. You think you be doing same foolish stuff you did years ago?"

I quickly answered. "Oh, no. I've learned but I still feel guilty. I sometime look back and wonder, 'What was that crazy person *thinking* back then?'"

Patting my hand she assured me, "You not be still feeling guilty. Those guilty feelings there when you make mistake to tell you not to do that anymore again. Once you learn that, you just stop the guilty stuff. It not help anymore. You just go on and be as kind and as good as you know how. You begin to balance. This why Grandmother come. She help balance."

Shelly sifted beach sand through her fingers as she asked, "Walt showed us the many forms that…ah…that he is. You were one of those forms."

Grandmother nodded and Shelly continued. "For years we've been hearing about visions of Mary, the mother of Jesus. These visions seem to have accelerated over the last ten years. She gives the same warning each time that we had better change our ways or we're in big trouble. Is this part of the female energy that you're talking about?"

Grandmother looked pleased as she said comfortingly, "Walt come as gentle, wise male energy. Grandmother come as farseeing female energy. Some people see Buddha, Jesus, other people see Mary, many people seeing what they call angels. All be touching people to bring balance and wisdom. All saying they not bringing religion, they bringing healing."

"Are people listening?" I asked.

"Some," she sighed heavily. "Maybe not enough. Maybe people have to go through hard time to finally listen, like silly children."

"Hard time? You mean all the predictions that we read about, the earth changes?"

In answer, she instructed us to close our eyes, breathe deeply and meditate. "After your mind quiet, you listen. Then you hear what Mother Earth be saying."

We did as she told us. After a few minutes I could hear the rhythm of the waves and that rhythm lulled me into a deep place. Then I heard a breathy voice, like a voice on the wind.

I open myself to all creatures. I pour myself out, giving, giving. I give of myself in joy for your life. I spill my waters upon you to cleanse and sustain you. My sun warms all living things, calling up life from the frozen ground.

I nourish you. I am Mother. Why do you destroy me? You fill my air and my waters with poisons. You open my belly and cut a grave for chemicals and radiation. You wound me with bombs. You destroy my forests, creating deserts. I love and feel only the trauma of your battles.

Awaken, my children, or in my anguish I will shake you from my skin. Bestir from your slumber of darkness and greed.

I'm dying. I weaken. I moan. My death rattle will rock me from my orbit. When I die, my children die, my children die, my children die...

The words faded but the chanting hum continued, throbbing mournfully with the ocean's pulse. The wind gusted strongly and seemed to cry warnings of storms to come. Slowly the sounds subsided. I opened my eyes and saw Grandmother, tears running down her dark and wrinkled cheeks. I was choked with emotion for Grandmother, for the earth whom we had treated so wretchedly.

I reached for Grandmother, enfolded her in my arms, wanting to soothe her grief. She patted my back and said in my ear, "You not cry for me. Cry for self, cry for other creatures, cry for Mother."

We knelt in the sand, Shelly, Grandmother and I, rocking each other to comfort while Grandmother hummed that crooning, flutelike melody. She released us, sat back on her heals, wiped her eyes with the hem of her shawl and said, "People must know old ways."

"Grandmother, that's impossible," I burst out, my eyes bright with tears. "We've come too far. People will never go back, give up their comforts and conveniences. Some of our progress has been positive like vaccines to prevent disease, education that helps stop poverty..."

Shelly added to my list, "You speak of the female side, Grandmother, look how far women have come. In our mother's and grandmother's youths it was against the law to practice birth control, women couldn't vote..."

Grandmother put her finger to her lips to quiet the onrush of our arguments. "Listen," she began, "it is to go back in spirit. In old ways women didn't have to fight for rights. They be powerful, strong. Men knew this. That was how things be. Then somewhere, sometime men decided there be God who was male. That be when things got all topsy-turvy. If *God* be male then males must be better. So men began to make all decisions and things get all out of balance. That too be part of evolution but then because it be *all* male energy they not see shadowside."

She stopped talking and watched as a flock of terns flew swiftly, skimming the water, silver wings magically flickering as they turned direction as one. Shelly asked, "What's shadowside?"

She gave us her attention when she answered, "That be part of all balance. Everything have two sides." She held up two fists and raised one. "*This*," she indicated with one raised fist, "be progress in medicine. Oh, great things happen. The vaccines, keeping things clean so no germs bring infections, anesthesia, all the operations that fix things inside that go wrong. These be good." Then she raised her other fist, "*This* be shadowside. People begin to see how these good things can cause problems. More and more people stay alive because of medicine. Too many people, not enough food, not enough houses, medicine cost go high, high, too high for people to pay. People be kept alive on machines, people that want to die because it be their time but law says no. Law says that would be murder. Everything have shadowside"

I thought of what she was saying and carried that truth to what I knew of today's other problems. All the things that were supposed to make our world a better place have brought problems that we don't know how to solve. Science's discovery of the atom gave us the bomb and later, nuclear power. Nuclear power was supposed to give us cheap, unlimited energy but where do we put the waste? Automobiles made us mobile yet look at the problems we now have because of that invention. Industry gave us a myriad supply of goods but polluted the world. Wherever progress trudged its way the old cultures were destroyed forever.

I drew patterns in the sand absentmindedly and asked, "Albert Einstein said that the problem is not in the atom bomb but in the hearts of the people. Is that what you mean by the shadowside?"

Nodding, she answered, "That be it. Albert, he knew. He be sad when he saw what men did with his wisdom. Everybody got to get together and listen to his wise words. They then discover old ways brings much happiness. At first, they be afraid if they give up stuff they not have good life. People think good life is in stuff, stuff they don't even need but it be in being close to Mother Earth."

"Will you tell us about the old ways, Grandmother?" Shelly asked wistfully.

She smiled warmly and drew her shawl around her shoulders as she began. "All ancient cultures knew balance. All knew life come from Mother Earth. All close to Mother and celebrate her seasons and all wonderful things Mother gave. In old ways elders have true wisdom. Today you have few wise elders. Oh, you have plenty old people but few *wise* old people. You not have wisdom all during life you not suddenly find it somewhere when hair be white. So, when things were in balance children gathered around the honored old ones, the white-hairs. Here they learn truths: passages of growth, lessons of bravery, strength, honor, courage, harmony. They had to pass tests to earn honor to be seen as giving members of tribe. *All* people in tribe were mothers and fathers to *all* tribe's children. No separation, like now. There be no rituals now so children know when they become adults. Children now make own rites of passage...that be gangs, drugs, playing with sex pleasures, driving the cars, drinking alcohol. They just don't know. They think these things make them grown up men and women.

"Men and women have to know that when they make baby they have most important job to do. Whole community, like tribe, have to know that little ones be responsibility of everyone. When children know love, know security, when they learn from wise elders then things begin to balance."

In alarm I exclaimed, "Grandmother! That will take generations! You've said that bad things are going to happen if we don't change. We can't wait until some generation a hundred years from now is wise!"

The sage old woman beamed, "*That* be why Walt be here, why Grandmother visit. *We* be elders to you. You gather around," she made a sweep with her hand, "and listen and learn. Just like old ways. This be happening all over planet. It speed things up but it still be up to all people. Spirit not be forcing anybody. We tell, you listen, you act."

"It would speed things up if you made a little visit to Washington," I muttered.

Grandmother just smiled.

Shelly and I burst out laughing and I asked, "Are you? Are our government leaders learning from you too?"

She raised a finger in warning. "Some. Most will never listen if I set fire under their fanny. They think they too important. Baaa, all ego stuff. But, yes, we visit some and they listen. Some people go to White House for own power. Some go because they love Mother Earth and people and they want to do good stuff. These be the ones we go to. It beginning."

"Do you think we can change before it's too late?" Shelly asked.

She waved her hand to dismiss the question, "Not what Grandmother think that matters now. What matters is what *you* think." She pointed at Shelly and at me.

Shelly drew back, "What *we* think? We don't have any power!"

Grandmother shook her head in exasperation. "That be your trouble! Everybody feel powerless. Women not know how powerful they be! What Walt tell you? He say we touch people with Light and Light go from heart to heart until it change whole world."

She poked Shelly's chest, "*This* where it begin. You change life, use less in world, use well, don't make mess on Mother. Be strong! Have honor! You keep love in heart and that love spread."

She sat quietly in thought for a time, then spoke again, "I know person who was great prophet. You call him Thoreau. He was man who saw ways of ancients. He say that Indian stand free in Nature, is her guest and wears her gracefully but civilized man is prisoner in house. Thoreau had old ways in heart. You need Thoreaus now."

She scowled fiercely and gazed out to sea.

I smiled. How was it possible that I felt such deep love for her, felt that I had known her forever as if she had been with me all my life and more? In one afternoon she had become so dear to me. Even in her severity I felt love. The way she spoke was endearing. A woman of her wisdom could easily speak English (or any language) clearly and perfectly. I suspect she spoke broken English because it was childlike and appealing.

Her eyes darted to me, "You think this be funny? This serious stuff here!"

I squeezed her hand. "I know, Grandmother. I just love you. You make me smile."

She pulled her shawl around her shoulders and muttered, "Hmm, you better start loving Mother Earth." Then she put her flute to her lips and began that same haunting music.

I closed my eyes and saw images of what was to come, flashes of changes. When my eyes opened the old enchantress was no longer with us on the beach but her music continued to breathe with the surf's ebb and flow. Shelly and I sat alone, travelers who had seen strange and distant places and were unable to find words to tell of the journey. We were both in our silent thoughts. Slowly we walked back through The Cliffs to where we had left the car. I felt I, not only I, but all life was teetering on the edge, at a crossroads and eternity was holding its breath, awaiting our decision.

René Donovan

Chapter 5

The Shadowside

The shadow, illusive, exists only on the other side of Light. Within the realm of shadow iciness slides, hollowness prevails and ignorance blinds like a sealed book. Within the shadow is trapped all that binds humankind within the dimension of pain.

The shadow sees not the Light but the Light has a voice and the voice is the word spoken across the void of the beginning. It was that which called out to the seeds of life. The seeds stirred and grew and clothed the earth in its breathing green mantle.

In our ignorance we hide in the shadows. In our blindness we have lived in the shadows and that darkness engulfs us in our poisoned prison.

Every innocent creature, every needing child, every green thing struggling to rise from the barren ground will look to us and ask, "Why?"

Can you fathom this...if we continue to turn from the Light we will return to the mute and silent void?

The weeks passed with no further contact from Walt or Grandmother. Shelly and I met often and deepened our friendship. We talked with Robert, Don and Jeff at the coffee shop, got to know them as friends and, I believe, if it weren't for each other we would all be doubting our sanity.

Spring, in all her greening glory had called the flowers and leaf buds from their winter sleep and the lengthening days were balmy. I began to work in my gardens, cleaning up the debris from winter storms and turning the soil for seeding. Out of necessity I had returned to my work in the studio and, except for the more creative aspects, my heart wasn't in it. The bills coming in didn't allow me to continue wandering the beaches and pondering life's questions but it was always there in the back of my mind: Grandmother, Walt, their words would echo in my head. While talking with a client who was intent on choosing the right color for a print job my mind would wander and I'd hear haunting remnants of Grandmother's flute or hear Walt's words, "I weep for my children!" The work I was doing in advertising seemed superficial, meaningless and yet I needed money to survive. I couldn't reconcile the two worlds: material, spiritual.

After a long week filled with frustrations I awoke to a beautiful Saturday morning. The sun's rising created long, deep patches of sunlight on the grass, the tops of the greening trees seemed translucent as the light filtered through the lacy foliage. The morning mists hung above the meadow—ghostly, swirling curls of golden, smoky air. The aroma of coffee brewing filled my home while I showered and dressed. Barefoot, I walked out onto the dewy grass with my cup of steaming coffee and sat at the picnic table holding my face up toward the sun. The air smelled faintly of lavender. It smelled green. Birds, back from their Southern vacation, chorused the air. Was it me, I wondered, or had the earth taken on an uncommon glow?

I breathed deeply, appreciating the combined aromas of coffee and the heady scents in the air only at springtime. My weekends were treasures which I guarded greedily. I seldom allowed anyone to guilt me into doing anything but enjoying but the phone was ringing and I left my outdoor temple to run inside to answer it. Shelly was as excited as I over the beautiful morning and invited me out to breakfast and for a long walk in the woods to a stream she knew of where the Lily of the Valley were beginning to bloom.

Later, I pulled into the parking lot of the coffee shop and when I entered I saw Shelly was already there, drinking coffee and chatting with Jeff, Robert and Don. I joined them at the booth and, after ordering breakfast, we were soon into one of our deep discussions.

Thinking we had a great adventure to share with them we related our story of Grandmother at the ocean. They listened, smiling all the while. "What?" I asked, somewhat offended. "You don't believe us?"

Jeff's beautiful dark face shone with excitement, big brown eyes glinting with mischief. "We went hiking up Mount Monadnock in New Hampshire, walked off the beaten path to do a little exploring and, just like you, we heard the flute. So we followed the sound and came to a clearing. There she was, sitting on a rock like she'd been waiting for us."

Robert added, "What she talked to us about was pretty much the same as with you. Except, her exact words were, 'You men stop acting like rooster all puffed up and ready for fight'" They laughed and agreed that sometimes they did act like roosters.

"Does that make you feel bad? I mean, both Walt and Grandmother keep talking about the male energy causing violence," Shelly questioned.

"Not really," Jeff answered, shaking his head. "They explain that it's balance we need. Grandmother said a strong man knows violence is weakness. It's true, you know. All the wars, the crime, it's all unbalanced energy. We sometimes act like Neanderthals dressed up for the 90s."

In getting to know Don, Robert and Jeff I realized they all had the same qualities in their lives: love of solitude, gentle manliness, love of nature. Jeff, Vietnam veteran, had learned the most extreme lesson about violence and had lived his life since the war in solitude, seeking nature and nurture. We called him the African American Thoreau for he lived in a tiny cottage in the woods. He was a carpenter by trade and had showed us photographs of some of the uniquely beautiful small home interiors he had designed and built.

Robert had been an activist against the war in the 60s and since that time had continued to be politically active against war and violence. He was a landscape architect and his home, though modest, was surrounded by absolutely palatial gardens. One got the feeling they were wandering in an enchanted, magical fairy garden, as perhaps they were.

Don, with his two older brothers, had inherited a commercial fishing boat from their father and spent long days at sea. It was a hard life, being at the mercy of the sea and its depleting resources, but he seemed to love the freedom of riding the waves in the open air, not bound by walls or office politics.

Above the smells of cooking and cigarette smoke I detected that wonderful aroma that always surrounded Walt and there was Himself, walking through the door, waving and smiling as if it were the most ordinary occurrence that he join us for breakfast. People stared at him for his appearance was anything but ordinary. Jeff slid over in the booth to make room for him and Judy, the waitress, arrived quickly, gazing at him as if she couldn't believe her eyes. It seemed that he would allow others to see him at times and at other times he was able to put a protective barrier around us.

"What can I get for you?" she asked Walt, pencil poised above the pad.

He touched her arm and answered enthusiastically, "Oh, my dear, if you please, I would enjoy a platter of scrambled eggs and maybe some potatoes with that and a big mug of coffee. That would be most kind, thank you."

Well, isn't this nice, I thought. Having breakfast with God. I stifled a giggle as the song ran through my head, "If they could see me now…" You don't tell your friends about things like this. How can you tell anyone that you meet God in the coffee shop? You don't. God is one of those folks people talk about but no one knows Him (or Her) personally. It's all theology, intellectual discussion, an abstract concept. No one says, "Jesus and his Dad stopped in the other night. We played cards." This is name-dropping taken to astronomical heights. People who make such claims are kept under close surveillance, under lock and key, even.

I began laughing, leaning against Shelly, covering my mouth with my hand. Everything suddenly struck me as enormously funny. It was definitely inappropriate laughter, like that macabre, nervous urge to laugh at a funeral.

Walt joined my laughter. "Oh," he sighed, "I know, Diana, I know. Communing with the Creator in church is appropriate but communing at breakfast? I fathom that most would see that as strange. Why, do you suppose, do people find it so difficult? When in church to whom do they pray?" He wasn't arguing. He seemed to be finding this tremendously amusing.

Jeff grumbled, "I think they pray because it's the expected thing in church. I doubt that most think they are actually talking to their Creator. Maybe they *hope* someone's listening."

Don asked, "Like prayer roulette."

Jeff nodded in agreement, "Or heaven insurance. Certainly won't hurt to give it a try."

Walt patted Jeff's hand and immediately Jeff's beautiful face broke into a smile. How can he do that, I wondered? How can just a touch cause us to feel so blissful?

"My people must mature the way they perceive God. Only when they realize that what they call God is not *apart* from them but a part *of* them, only then will they comprehend prayer.

"Prayer or meditation is not demanding, making deals or groveling. It is communicating, listening. In prayer you open to that which is life. It is acknowledging that which is *within*." He touched Jeff's chest with the tips of his fingers. "Your bodies and minds have been created with powers so awesome, so wondrous. Do you realize that laughter releases healing chemicals and that tears release chemicals that relieve stress? Every cell in your body is replaced within a period of seven years. The body that was yours seven years ago is not the body that you live in now. Can you grasp the implications of this?

"Oh, my people, awaken. Open your eyes. Dare to look through that thin veil that seems to separate us. The Creator holds out arms to you, waiting. Miracles are given and await your acceptance."

Robert took his glasses off and wiped them on a napkin. He replaced them and adjusted them on his nose then asked, "Miracles? You mean like healing and visions?"

"Need you look for that which is out of the ordinary? *Life* is a miracle! Miracles are all around you." He made a grand sweep with his arms. "Thinking is a miracle, as is birth, the seasons, instinct. Who tells the birds when it is time to fly south? Who shows them when and how to build nests for their young? What is it within all growing things that knows the progress of the seasons? Within the bulb of a spring flower is all the knowledge of its blooming. Without instruction, animal and plant life is in touch with the Source. As humans, with your reasoning minds you have intellectualized yourselves from a primal knowing, from a birthright of joy but it is there, waiting. You have only to receive."

He paused, as if to allow the words to penetrate our blocked minds. I wanted to hear more of his words, words spoken not in preaching or condescension, but in gentleness and love. I felt a thirst, a hunger for this magic.

"The stars and moon in the limitless sky are there and you barely notice. How many people walk into the night and gaze up at the night-sky and feel that it is proof enough that there is more than just a life of struggle?"

When he paused I looked around and noticed that other people were listening to him and the old man named George was among them. I remembered that he was one of the people that I had listened to so many weeks ago. Was it only weeks? It seemed like years since I had sat here writing so negatively and overhearing the conversation about the "Bloody Night in Boston."

George caught my eye, got up from the stool and walked over to us. "Name's George," he said, while he held out his hand to each of us as we introduced ourselves. When he shook Walt's hand, as it happened with everyone, a look of surprised delight crossed his face. "Mind if I join you? Couldn't help but overhear your conversation. Interesting."

Walt was pleased that George was there. "Please. Please sit, join us."

Shelly and I squeezed together so that George would have room to sit. Our little group was growing. Would everyone in the coffee shop soon try to squeeze into our booth?

"Didn't mean to eavesdrop but what you were saying just caught my attention. You a preacher?" George asked.

Walt's eyes crinkled as he laughed and shook his head, "Oh, my, no! I'm just a visiting friend."

He leaned back in the booth and asked, "Has anyone ever told you, sir, that you are a dead ringer for Walt Whitman?"

Walt nodded, smiling, and answered, "That has been brought to my attention."

George paused for a moment, staring at Walt thoughtfully, then continued. "Philosophy's kind of a thing with me, read everything I can get my hands on. Spiritual things too, though I don't belong to a church. I guess you could call me a questioning agnostic."

Walt seemed pleased. "Oh, it's the *questioning* minds that seek and find."

"I liked what you said about going out and looking at the night sky. Why, that's a real show! One of these days I'd like to get myself a telescope so I can get right out there. Nature is something, ain't she? Now, to me, that's God. *That* I can know, can speak to and it speaks to me."

Will Walt take him on the cosmic tour? He won't need a telescope if he hangs around here.

"Well, of course it does!" Walt exclaimed. "Oh, that more people would listen. Those that listen are the true artists. They receive the Creator through their creations. What you perceive as God comes to them to write the symphonies, to paint the pictures, to write the poems. The Creator enters the hearts and the lives of those questioning and gives them new life."

His words were musical, were poetry. I was listening intently but began feeling that odd intuition we sometimes experience when something is not quite right, that chill on the back of the neck and then I looked from Walt and saw him.

The face of the man in my dream. He was sitting at the counter facing us and what I saw in his eyes was like looking into a storm. He rose from his seat and slowly approached us. Walt stopped talking and everyone faced the intruder. I could read nothing in Walt's eyes of his feelings about this man. There was only a quiet calm in him.

The man leaned on the table and hissed, *"How can you speak of such evil things?"*

"What are you talking about?" George defended. "He said nothing evil!"

He pointed at George, "You! You said *nature* is your God. And you," he turned to Walt, "teaching that we're *part* of God Almighty." He held up a shaking finger and lowered his voice. "There was only one...only one who was part of the Almighty and that was his only son, our Lord, Jesus Christ. How *dare* you presume to say you are like our Savior?"

My mouth was open in horror that anyone would speak to gentle Walt with such hatred. I was furious! "Listen here, if you only knew…"

Walt held up a hand to silence me. "My friend, if you please, let us speak calmly. I meant not to offend your beliefs."

I thought the man was going to explode. "You're no friend of mine! *My* beliefs? These are the beliefs of all good Christians. Our Lord came to us and died for our sins and believing that is the *only* way we'll be saved! Not by believing that God is in the *stars*." He spat the words out like venom, spun on his heals and left, shoving aside some people who'd been standing by the door.

The morning's joy was tarnished as if the sun were eclipsed. "What a good Christian," I muttered.

The waitress brought our breakfasts. She looked disturbed, as if she wanted to ask us what had happened. When she left, Walt took a drink of his coffee and advised us, "Enjoy, enjoy. You must not allow what is in him to come upon you."

"How can you just let it go?" Robert questioned. "Oh, I hate those kinds of people."

Walt stopped eating and looked at Robert with sadness in his eyes. "Oh, no, Robert. Do not hate. The man felt threatened. That is all."

"Sorry," Robert mumbled. "You're right, of course. I don't really *hate* them. I just get angry that some people can be so narrow-minded."

"And he feels angry that you don't agree with his beliefs. That is how wars begin."

"I may disagree with him but I wouldn't barge in on him the way he did to us. I can accept his beliefs I just don't want them forced on me."

"That is your way. This was his. There will come a time in his evolution when he will see clearer."

Robert shrugged, "I hope I don't meet up with him again. If he starts in I don't know if I could hold my temper."

Walt shook his head slowly and sadly, saying, "Violence will never bring peace."

George folded his hands on the table, old, spotted hands that had toiled for over eighty years. "He's right, Robert. Every night on the news you can see the results of people who just won't agree and they think they can solve their disagreements with violence."

Walt put aside his fork, wiped his mouth on his napkin and said, "The violence taking place in the world is like a wound upon the earth, coming to a head, cleansing itself. Humanity has evolved through century after century from a consciousness of survival to what you are today. That savage consciousness is still within you and your society is now facing the results of this. People throw their hands up in helplessness and see no answers because the answers lie in the next evolution, of going beyond what is seen and exploring the unseen."

I listened to his words but that man kept stealing into my thoughts. I remembered the dream. After Grandmother had given me the urn and I turned to walk away, he was there, waiting and watching on the hill. Forcing myself to release those thoughts I turned my attention back to my companions.

Jeff was questioning Walt about religion, obviously regarding our angry intruder. "The man was very firm in his beliefs but it seems to me there was a definite lack of the compassion that Jesus and others taught."

"This sometimes happens," Walt nodded. "There is truth in the core of all religions which are but spokes around the wheel of the Creator. Truths are often given to those who cannot comprehend their simplicity. They constrict a Creator as untouchable, unreachable, unknowable. They teach you to love God but how can you love what you do not *know*? Religion often teaches you to have blind faith. Blind faith can lead to the horror that was seen in the mass suicide at Jonestown and to mindless sheep following the blind rages of a dictator that resulted in the torture and death of millions in the Holocaust.

"Faith, my friends, comes through the search, through experiencing, through observation. Oh, my dear friends, can you not see? Observe your world and see that all life shows you the way. It points to the interrelatedness of all things. It sings that there is more than merely a life of struggle. *Life!*" he crooned, the word hanging over us like the note of a symphony. "My people take it so for granted. To truly and deeply observe yourselves and your planet carries you to faith, not in dogmas and dead teachings, but faith in the Source that created it all. Faith is in the mystery that is observable yet often seemingly invisible."

We waited, mesmerized, for him to continue but he gazed out the window next to us as if deep in thought. Then, smiling broadly, he said, "Come, if you please. Let us leave now. This morning is much too beautiful to not be part of it."

We struggled out of the booth and I reached into my purse for my billfold but Walt stilled my hand and said, "That is not necessary." We looked back at the table and there, on the check that the waitress had left, was a neat stack of bills.

I looked at Walt, amused and questioning. "That surprises you?"

he asked. "Where do you think money comes from?"

Robert burst out laughing and answered, "I've prayed for that plenty of times but never expected it to happen."

As we were leaving Walt said, "Money is but an agreed upon form of exchange. In back of all prosperity is the Creator."

We thanked him for his kindness and I pondered on how many gifts I've received over my lifetime and had never thought to say "Thank you." I guess that when we receive we think it is just our due or we credit it to good luck.

We walked through the door and the sun poured upon us. Everything sparkled. I felt as if it were the first morning of creation like the words of an old hymn, "Morning has broken, like the first morning…" Was it really this beautiful or was it the company? Walt and Grandmother seemed to have opened me, given me new sight, fresh insights.

Knowing them also gave me heightened intuition and despite all the beauty of the morning I felt that something was wrong. Walt stood beside me and said in a low voice, "Did Grandmother not tell you that there is a shadowside?" Sensing the charged atmosphere, the others gathered around us, waiting for Walt to explain.

Then we heard the voice of that man calling. "I'll stop you! I won't let you spread your lies! God will show me the way!"

I looked up at Walt but he only stood there, his face filled with patience and compassion, watching the man standing beside his car with a raised fist. "Walt, who *is* he?" I asked.

Walt smiled sadly, "His name is Leonard."

"I mean, *who is he*?" I insisted.

Robert glanced at Leonard over his shoulder and laughed nervously. "If you tell us he's the devil himself I'll believe it. Man, that guy's got problems."

"Devil?" Walt asked. "You know there is no such entity. Satan is but a name people have given to what they see as evil and evil is but ignorance."

"What's he going to do?" George asked.

"Exactly what he has said, try to stop us," Walt answered.

"Can he do that?" I gasped.

Walt looked at me, surprised. "Diana, he has free will as all do."

"But can't you stop him? I mean...you're…"

He shook his head. "I am not a tyrant, a dictator. You invited me so I am here. He does not invite me so I cannot interfere. I can only wait for him to receive."

"What will he do to us?" Shelly questioned, fear in her voice.

"What you allow."

Ordinarily, I could ignore a man such as Leonard but he seemed crazy enough to carry through on his threat. My intuition cautioned me to tread very carefully as one would when hearing the rattle of a snake.

We left the parking lot and began walking, following Walt through the intersection, down the main street and turning left onto a winding, hilly side road that led to the North River. Walt eased himself up on the stone wall of the bridge which crossed over the river, miles and miles of brackish water which eventually fed into the ocean. Along its grassy banks grew willow, birch, oak and maple trees—a splendid array of color especially when autumn dipped her brush in the vibrant palette or reds, yellows and russets. But now, in spring, the varied shades of greens and yellows were like a watercolor wash against the deep, dark blackness of the water.

I leaned against the wall next to Walt and while he was talking to Shelly, Robert, Don, George and Jeff my mind drifted back to the scene with Leonard. Am I just filling up my worry space or is his threat something I should take seriously. It's that damned dream that causes me such dread, I thought.

Walt, who always seemed to know when we were troubled, leaned over to me and whispered, "It is time to leave that path."

I looked at his face, into his eyes that sparkled below the brim of his hat. "What path?"

"The path of fear. Look back upon your life and see where that fear has led you. To be cautious is wise. To be fearful is ignorance of Who you are."

"How can I know if I'm being fearful or cautious?" I asked, troubled.

He placed his hand on my forehead then on my stomach. "You feel the difference here. What are you feeling now?"

I concentrated on the two places he was touching and tried to sort through the emotions. "I'm feeling a tightness, sort of nauseous." I closed my eyes. "I want to hide from Leonard. I dread something he may do to me...to us."

"When you remember Leonard's threat do you feel in control of your life? Do you feel connected to Who you are?" he questioned gently.

"No. Definitely not."

"Do you feel like a victim?"

I placed my hand over my stomach when he said those words, as if to comfort myself. "Yes! That's it exactly. Being threatened made me feel like a victim."

"Do you think you have control over how you feel?"

Cautiously, I answered, "Well, the older I get the less I allow myself to be victimized. I've learned that being a victim has no rewards. Self pity gets really boring. Yes, I do have control. It's just that sometimes when I'm scared it's hard to remember that."

Robert, Don and Jeff listening to our conversation had the same reaction. Robert spoke up. "When someone threatens me I don't get afraid. I get angry." Don and Jeff nodded in agreement.

Walt hopped off the wall, supple as a boy and walked over to Robert, placing his big hands on Robert's forehead and stomach. "What are you inner emotions when you are angry?"

Robert was silent as he obviously tried to dredge up the sensations of his anger. His face reddened when he replied, "I'm feeling fearful."

Jeff looked askance at Robert and argued, "But they're not the same thing! Fear is running away and anger is...protecting, standing up for yourself."

"Anger is fear and that kind of fear leads to violence."

Jeff insisted, "Not if you don't act on it."

Walt, ever patient with us, answered calmly, "To act upon it is violence to another, to *feel* it is violence to the *self*. When you feel anger acknowledge it, observe it and allow it to pass."

"But Walt," Robert argued, "what if someone came into your house and was going to hurt your children? You mean to tell me that I should just stand there and let it happen?"

Walt shook his head slowly and just stared at Robert until he began to fidget uncomfortably. "This is the most misunderstood concept that comes to the lives of my people. Think!" Walt said emphatically.

We looked at him blankly, thick as bricks. His eyes focused on each of us, silently asking if we understood.

"Have I not told you of your power? Have I not said that you are part of the Creator?"

Shelly nervously asked, "But isn't that contradictory? If we have power over others that in itself can lead to violence."

"Power over others? No, it is power within the self. It is interior. When you know of your own power there is no desire for power over others."

"How then," Robert asked, "do you protect yourself from others who *are* violent?"

Walt smiled. He remained so untiring with us. This reminded me of the stories in the New Testament when Jesus would be speaking to the people and he had to resort to storytelling, to parables because the ignorance of the people didn't allow them to understand.

Cars occasionally drove over the bridge, slowing down to stare at the strange gathering standing by the wall. Finally, it began to dawn on me what Walt was saying. "I got it!" I yelled.

Everyone turned in my direction as if I had lost my senses. I waved my hands like a crazy woman. I thought for a moment before I could voice what I was understanding. "When you get to the point in your growth where you feel so totally secure...no, no it's deeper than that..." I grimaced in frustration.

Walt smiled in sympathy. Then he said the words which stunned us all.

"When you get to the point in your growth when you know that… *you...are...God"* his gaze traveled around the group, "you will be *incapable* of feeling fear or anger. Knowing Who you are allows you the wisdom to create your own life."

The shock of those words and the authority with which they were spoken jolted us. I was pulled back from the location, and as I traveled in my mind, the words, "Incapable of fear, incapable of fear," traveled with me.

My eyes opened. I was sitting at the picnic table in my back yard, sloshing coffee from my cup down my arm. I glanced at my watch, shocked to realized that no time had passed since I sat here at, what seemed to be, early morning.

Immune now to these surprises, I continued sitting at the picnic table, sipping coffee and contemplating my journey. I didn't understand how these little sojourns occurred, whether they were all in our minds, or if Walt and Grandmother could call us to another dimension in time. Could it be, as in the ancient lore of Avalon, that mists carry me from the present to an enchanting holy place? I only knew they were real, perhaps more real than sitting in my back yard on a Saturday morning. I began to think of all that happened with Walt and Grandmother as the Dreamtime and I knew the Dreamtime was a reality.

René Donovan

Chapter 6

The Circle

There is a place where all possibilities lie, a quantum journey through the mists of nighttime. There is a time of no moments, a blink with no before and no after; a vibrating, luminous question. There are nights of such mystical momentum that only those with eyes that see through all life have the ability to unfold the path leading through the mists to encounter the Circle.

Draw your cloak close around your shoulders, step out into the night and into the magic. Follow the nightstilled path through the forest where hallowed places await.

Spring swelled into summer, giving me gifts of pink, blue and white morning glories trailing up the stone planters on either side of my front door. Silvered dew was caught in the cup of each flower-trumpet. Mother Earth opened herself and my flower gardens were heavy with blossoms, birds and butterflies which fanned their colorful wings in the sun. So rich were the colors the gardens seemed embroidered from an impressionist's palette. The strawberry patch was red with fruit, the vegetable garden so heavily laden with perfect ripening specimens that the vines and branches bent to the ground. Winter seemed a lifetime ago.

Grandmother had taught me to commune with my garden from

the first blessed seeds laid within the awakening soil to the time of harvest. She said that Mother Earth hears your thoughts, she receives your thoughts. As I worked I softly sang and sent warmth and nurturing to each tiny sprout. Grandmother told me which phase of the moon in which to plant each seed and it was clear that her advice held truth for even my cats seemed to cherish this delightful spot. They daily lazed among the thick foliage of squash, tomatoes and green beans so that sometimes it was difficult to find cat under leaf. During the growing season their fur smelled of sun and lavender.

    I had worked most of the afternoon in the garden and was tired when I finally took my work gloves off and went into the house, three kitties trailing behind me. They immediately dashed to their bowls. One of their unshakable convictions is that a bowl should never remain devoid of yummies and if they look into a bowl that doesn't hold some tidbit they'll frown and stare as if they can't quite believe their eyes. What actors cats are! They can turn the most ordinary of happenings into an academy award performance. If they could manage it, cats would wear costumes and go on stage. I sprinkled dry food into the dish under their noses as they hunkered down and watched the morsels fall with happy interest.

    The day was June 21, the Summer Solstice, also known as Midsummer Night. Summer Solstice has always been a favorite time of year for me because it celebrates the longest day of the year, a day when summer is at her fullest and ripest. I was pleasantly anticipating honoring Mother Earth tonight in the company of Robert, Don, Jeff, George and Shelly. I had already make a quiche so all I had to do was make a salad later.

    I was looking forward to creating the "ceremonial grounds" in the nearby woods. After washing up and having a quick lunch I went to the shed where I found my rake and grass clippers then followed the narrow path, cushioned with pine needles, leading through the woods until it opened to a clearing where sun and shade dappled the forest floor under towering oaks, maples and pines. This was the place where I'd made a sort of campsite when my children were small, where we'd come on hot summer nights, build a fire in a circle of rocks, cook hamburgers, roast marshmallows and tell stories. The circle of rocks was still there, years after the children were grown and I could almost feel their tired little bodies leaning sleepily against me as I helped them to hold their marshmallow sticks out of the flames.

The earth had begun reclaiming this circle, sending briars up to entangle saplings and bushes. I clipped them back then raked all around the circle to prevent sparks from igniting the dried pine needles and to create a smooth place for us to sit upon. How quickly the forest takes back what is hers, I thought as I gathered wood that had fallen from the surrounding trees during the winter and made a huge stack for the night's campfire. The forest is like the ocean, which eventually claims her shores from the presumptuousness of human building.

Earlier that morning while on my round of errands I had bought several wind chimes, those wonderfully tinkling, inexpensive glass ones imported from Japan. I hung them from low branches and as the soft, balmy breezes breathed through the forest they made an appealing tinkling that reminded me of ice cubes in a glass of lemonade. After I tied colored ribbons with flowing streamers from the trees' branches—pink, yellow, orchid, blue and white, I sat cross-legged on the ground to rest and admire the fairyland I had created with Mother Earth. Tired from my day's work, I lay back on the ground and stared up at the tops of the swaying trees, my mind drifting.

I thought about the past weeks and of the harassment all of us were experiencing from our good pal Leonard. He had begun to follow us when we drove and, out of nowhere, would show up and just stare. The first time I encountered him was at the grocery market. I had finished my shopping and came back to my car, opened the trunk and saw him parked next to me, his window open. His thinning gray hair was carefully combed to one side in an attempt to hide an obvious bald spot, his face gray with deep, puffy bags under his eyes. There was a hard, dissipated edge to him. Squinting at me through the sunlight, his eyes were almost serpentine in their lack of warmth. The shirt he wore was opened at the neck and I noticed that he wore a chain with a wooden cross hanging from it, about two inches in length with a silver lightning bolt running diagonally across it. When he saw that I had noticed, his fingers encircled it and, holding it out to the length of the chain, he smiled and drawled, "His countenance was like lightning and his raiment white as snow."

He spoke the quotation in singsong and I felt an absurd compulsion to continue it with, "...and everywhere that Mary went, the lamb was sure to go." I packed my groceries into the trunk of the car and left quickly, trying not to show the fear I was feeling. My hands shook on the wheel as I drove away, looking into the rear view mirror to see if he was following. He made me feel nauseous, contaminated, like I had touched an unimaginably warped, slimy side of humanity. Even after I had driven away I noticed that the smell of him lingered in the car. It was a heavy stink of men's cheap cologne splashed liberally onto an unwashed body. It probably had an exotic name like "Squalid."

A few days later when I came home from a business meeting there was an envelope taped to my front door. When I opened it a single piece of paper fell out and fluttered to the doorstep. As I bent down to retrieve it the words jumped out at me: "Woe unto them that call evil good, and good evil." He knew where I lived. That night Robert called telling me of the verse he'd found on his door: "And I will punish the world for their evil, and the wicked for their iniquity, and I will cause the arrogance of the proud to cease, and will lay low the haughtiness of the terrible." This man was psychotic and he knew where we all lived.

We decided they were too threatening to ignore but when we showed them to the police we were told that he'd have to commit a crime before they could do anything. All we had were the two notes and his description—no name, no address. In my haste to get away from him I had neglected to get his license number. They kept copies of the notes and said they'd watch for someone of his description in the area and asked that we call if we had any further information.

It was alarming. I felt I was always being watched, even here in my peaceful fairyland. Maybe I should look into finding me a dog, a monstrous critter about the size of a bull who wouldn't hesitate to hastily impale any sly rascal concealed in the shadows. I understood now why people got guns and kept them by their bedsides. Oh, right. I'd hear someone skulking about and end up blowing my toes into next week. Good God, was I going to end up being one of those pathetic creatures who constantly call the police late at night to report a man hiding under her bed?

I sat up on my elbows and looked around. Was he watching me now? My imagination took over and I saw Leonard creeping about in the bushes. He's probably the leader of some militant religious cult whose slogan is "Kill for Christ." I had visions of crazed fanatics chasing me through the woods with burning torches yelling, "Burn the witch!" Whoof! It was easy for Walt and Grandmother to talk. Ol' Leonard and his gang comes after them all they'd have to do is up and disappear leaving Leonard holding his torch.

I was scaring myself out here alone in the woods. Okay, calm down. Walt had told us that to control our fear we must focus and center. Can I, as he advised, be cautious without experiencing the crippling fear? Caution implies being vigilant when danger approaches but then to know our own power in the face of danger and to act calmly and wisely.

I sat up, calmed my mind and began to meditate, consciously loosening the tightened muscles in my neck and shoulders, then bringing my attention to my stomach, the third chakra, or energy point where emotions are stored. I placed my hand over the area to soothe and comfort and when I experienced a diminishing of tension I began to focus on the area of my forehead between my eyes. Walt taught us that this is the sixth chakra, called the Third Eye, and correlates with the pineal gland in the brain. The Third Eye is the chakra through which we physically receive enlightenment, the ability to see clearly.

As I eased down into another world, phantoms of colors swirled, carrying me away, rolling me in clouds. I was walking through a dark forest in which gnarled, intertwining roots reached out, tripping me. The darkness was not mysterious but murky, threatening and felt slimy on my skin. I walked alone, naked, holding nothing in my hands, nothing to use as a weapon against whatever was *out there waiting*. Mile after mile I trudged in this nightmare forest, this place where there was neither friend nor any other living creature. The trees themselves were dead stunted things, their empty branches overhead so thickly entangled they wove a tunnel through which I was pulled by something which was beyond my understanding. There was not a sound beyond my own labored breathing.

Ahead I glimpsed the beginning of a clearing which allowed a sickly orange glow of light to filter down and reflect off what appeared to be water and as I approached I gagged at the hideousness of what had been done to Mother Earth. The edges of the swamp bubbled under my bare feet, exuding a stench that had to be lethal and as I gazed out ahead of me this fathomless pit went on for seemingly miles. It's surface was lifeless, covered in sludge, feces...oily and thick and waiting and I knew I had to step forward and enter it.

The liquid stung my feet, sucked them down. I slid and fell, scrambling to remain upright. I cried out, begged for release but in the limited knowledge of dreams where logic is sidestepped, I knew I had to go on. The liquid rose upon me as I continued, up to my knees, my waist. *Things* slid around my ankles, horrors that were able to exist in this poisonous mire. I pushed aside the feces floating on the swamp's surface, crying, telling myself to take just one more step, one more, one more.

As in dreams, time was distorted. I could have endured for minutes, hours or days. It seemed forever before I saw the hard ground on the other side. I emerged and stood, leaning against the nearest tree, my eyes closed, gritting my teeth to keep the screams inside. Then I felt a soft, cleansing breeze flutter upon my body. I heard one bird's call. Through the rough bark of the tree I felt an energy pulsating. I opened my eyes. I was no longer naked but wore a long, black robe of a soft, light, woolen material, flowing down my body to my bare feet. Its full, draping hood covered my head. The tree on which I had leaned was now an oak staff in my hand, strong, sturdy, able to support me and upon it was carved ancient runes which I knew to be symbols of strength. Without looking back I strode from the dark forest into the sunlight, leaning on my staff, clean, strong and wise.

Meditation had carried me far from my home and when I opened my eyes it created a feeling that I had traveled long and distant but the message I'd received was clear: the only way to now solve life's problems is to bravely walk through the shit because when you get to the other side you'll be wiser and stronger. I smiled at the literal manner the vision showed this but wondered if I should interpret it as a warning that Leonard was planning to throw some nasties my way.

Despite the warm sunshine, I shivered, then got up and walked back to the house.

Later my friends began to arrive and as the late afternoon sun lowered into long shadows and streams of yellow over the lawn, we strolled around the yard. I was happy sharing my gardens, identifying herbs and answering questions about their uses. Robert fingered the leaves of a five foot tall plant and asked, "Is this an herb? I'm familiar with most of them but I…"

I stood from picking weeds, a never-ending task, and interrupted his question. "Oh, that's angelica. Isn't she a beauty? People in ancient Europe believed it protected against disease and evil. The stems can be cut up to make a sort of candy, it can be used medicinally to cure bladder and kidney problems or to soothe nausea." I fluffed up its foliage, causing the huge flower heads to bob under their weight and send out a sweet aroma.

The earth smelled ripe as we walked on and Robert bent down to touch some plants in my kitchen garden. George pressed in close and identified them. "I remember these. My wife used to grow them out by our back door. Let's see if I can name them…" he paused. "That one…that's oregano, that's thyme." He crushed a leaf between his fingers and brought it to his nose, "Oh, this is basil. Great stuff, basil."

I walked ahead and called to Shelly, "You'll be interested in this one."

She inspected the large, hairy leaf I extended to her and smiled questioningly. "It's comfrey," I said. "One of its uses is to soothe bruises and sprains. Farmers used to crush the leaves and make poultices for their horses' sprained legs. It was also known as knitbone. You could use it in massage therapy. The next time you come I'll cut a bunch for you. You can dry it and use it as a tea also."

Before we walked back to the house I picked basil, oregano and thyme to add to our salad, smiling as their wonderful scents rushed up to greet me. Once indoors we began preparations for supper. George showed us the beautiful label on a bottle of wine he had brought. Through the bottle its color was pale as autumn roses. "See this?" he asked, proudly. "I got this a vineyard in Rhode Island. Can you believe it? Rhode Island! Oh, it was just beautiful there, a little town right by the ocean. Owned by a family who used to live in New York City. Got sick of city living and bought the vineyard. Knew nothing about growing grapes or making wine but they learned and have a fine, prosperous business now. Nice way to make a living, don't you think?"

We decided that the fine wine should be chilled and sampled and an hour later while waiting for quiche Lorraine to warm in the oven we sat on the screened-in porch toasting to our newfound friendship, to Walt and Grandmother and the wonderful things we were learning.

While my friends sat and talked I went into the kitchen, took the quiche out of the oven and then set the table. Earlier, I had made an arrangement of peony blossoms and white votive candles floating in a wide, crystal bowl filled with water. I placed it in the center of the lace-covered dining room table, lit the candles and stood back to enjoy the mysterious, Victorian affect, filled with contentment. There is something so basically satisfying in sharing a meal with good companions. The night was warm, fitting for Midsummer Eve, and the sun was reluctant to set. Outside, amid the dusk, the treetops were aflame with russet gold, seeming to sink into the very leaves it set upon. I turned from the window as these good people began to come into the room: Robert, Shelly, Don, Jeff and George, their eyes alight with the beauty they encountered there. As if entering a church they sat quietly around the table and George held out a chair for me after I brought the quiche and salad to the table, giving me a smile and a nod as if in thanking me for this enchantment.

"If I may," Robert began, and turned to me, "I'd like to say grace with a Native American smudging." He withdrew a plastic bag from his shirt pocket, opened it's contents and we waited. "Do you have an ashtray?" he asked. I left and came back with the ashtray and as I handed it to him he continued. "Sage. The Native Americans used dried sage in their spirit cleansing ceremonies." He lit a match and held it to the leaves in the ash tray and when they began to catch and smoke he waved his hand over them, scooped the aromatic smoke into his palm and drew it from his heart region then over the top of his head. He handed it to Jeff, who did as Robert had shown, and as it went around the table's circle it's sweet pungent aroma like autumn leaves burning, filled the room. Candlelight-etched glasses were raised and Robert offered, "May our lives continue on the Mystery Walk."

The process of friendship is an intertwining one, slowly carrying someone through your history, into what made you what you are. So as we sat around the table, candlelight creating warmth and intimacy, we told tales of our lives, inviting each other to step into our journeys.

Shelly and I accepted the men's offer to clear the table and do the dishes while we readied the ceremonial grounds. We smeared our bodies with citronella oil, Shelly picked up a bag of candles she'd brought and with the flashlight beam to guide us, headed through the back yard and onto the path. We were silent as we traveled through the woods, listening to the night sounds and when we came to the clearing I touched a lighter to the dried leaves within the fire circle. They immediately caught the flame, the flame fed the kindling and within minutes our campfire was crackling. The fire opened the area like a shelter within darkness and Shelly stood smiling at the magic within the circle. The ribbons waved with the night's breeze and wind chimes played their soft melody. Shelly dropped the votive candles in their tiny red glass holders and placed them on the ground by a huge rock just outside the circle where they were protected from the breeze. Once lit, their flames added to the esoteric atmosphere, giving us the feeling that anything was possible on this night.

We sat cross-legged by the firelight and Shelly asked, "What do you have planned for us?"

"I haven't planned anything beyond this." I waved my hand around the area. "I thought that we'd just leave things loose and see what happens. Maybe we'll just sit and talk, maybe somebody will come up with a good idea."

"Maybe Grandmother and Walt will come," Shelly whispered.

I smiled, confiding, "Yeah, I was thinking about that while I was out here earlier but they seem to pop up when least expected so I don't want to get my hopes up."

As we sat chatting by the firelight we heard the men's voices and as they came into sight Jeff waved a large thermos at us. "I brought my special blend of coffee. Fresh beans. I thought it would be good to enjoy a cuppa' out here." Don trailed behind him carrying a tray of mugs, cream, sugar and spoons.

"Oh, how thoughtful," I cried. "You guys are great." They agreed that they were, indeed, great as they poured and served. As we made yummy noises over our coffee Robert showed us the Indian drum he had brought and explained that he had learned drumming from a men's healing circle in Arizona and would like to offer his talent to tonight's celebration. George offered to sing but after a brief sampling of his vocal ability we all agreed that he should not endanger his fantastic voice singing in the night air. He grumbled that great people were never appreciated in their own time, as he opened a beach chair he'd carried with him and lowered himself into it with a contented sigh. He was enjoying himself tremendously as the elder of our group. He was a wise man and one we all respected.

As the night deepened and the stars and moon bloomed through the lacy overhanging branches, fireflies danced in the woods like tiny sprites come to pay homage to Mother Earth. Strange sounds from remote places in the invisible forest told us that nocturnal animals, the night walkers, roamed. Truly, this was a sacred site and, oh, how we need places like this in our lives, lives often so barren of mystery.

At last we were seated in a circle around the fire and Robert began drumming. The ancient rhythm pounded with my bloodstream, my heart's beat. Shelly joined in with her clear, beautiful voice, we followed her example and it seemed that energy was being raised as the wind picked up, chimes adding to our music. In this timeless atmosphere I heard Grandmother calling, that eerie, somehow sad, breathing of her flute. Her music was from all nature: it was trees sighing, waterfalls rushing, streams gurgling, wolves howling, snow falling, thunder rolling, lions purring, children laughing, mockingbirds singing, wings fluttering, infants cooing, women weeping. The very stars kept rhythm with her song-spell.

Out of the deep, enshrouding forest came Walt and Grandmother, walking together, their magnificent images causing me to catch my breath. We stood to greet them and they held out their arms to us. It was then that we noticed that behind them stood the mother and child from the accident, the two that Walt had healed on that phenomenal stormy night. Grandmother and Walt each held out one arm to enfold them, drawing them into the group.

Grandmother's face was soft with love as she looked down at the child. "This be Emily," she told us.

The mother, beaming within the circle of Walt's arms, nodded toward us as Walt said, "And this is Emily's mother Dorothy."

Everyone began speaking at once, bombarding them with questions. Grandmother drew her shawl around her, lowered herself to the ground by the fire and gestured that we join her. "Many questions. Pretty soon we tell you all." She wore a crown of wildflowers upon her head, beautiful strings of beads around her neck and her dress was long and of the softest tan leather beaded around the neckline and hem. Around her shoulders she wore the black shawl I'd seen her wear before. She seemed delighted with her festive appearance and each graceful movement she made sent forth the exotic scent of sandalwood, cinnamon and apples. I smiled as my eyes fell upon Walt who wore a rosebud pinned to his white smock and stars and moons were painted in glittery silver upon his dear face. His long, gray hair blew wildly in the wind and I recalled the name people had long ago given Whitman: "The good, gray poet."

Emily's face was radiant as she gazed about the circle, firelight creating a halo around her copper curls and she leaned against Grandmother in familiar intimacy. "Everyone know about accident when Emily and Dorothy be healed," Grandmother began, her wonderful voice an invitation to magic. "That night while they be in hospital we go to them in dream and tell about journey they were about to take. We tell them Who we be, why we come to them." She held her hands out to us. "Just like we do for each of you."

Her voice was magic, like an ancient storyteller mesmerizing the tribe's people, striking a deep primeval chord within us. "These two be special people. Emily knew us. She be so close to Creator she not forget. Dorothy be afraid at first, just like you." She glanced at us mischievously and we nodded, acknowledging our initial dread. "But Emily talk with her. Emily tell her, 'You not have to be afraid. They be friends.' That be right, little one?" Grandmother nuzzled Emily's hair with a kiss.

Emily's sweet voice agreed, "Mama didn't know about the Happy People." She looked from Walt to Grandmother, then held Grandmother's hand. "That's what I called you when I only dreamed about you. Happy People, because you always came into my dreams and talked with me and you were always happy." She smiled shyly. "And you made me happy."

I felt tears come to my eyes. A little child shall lead them, indeed. Grandmother glanced at me and nodded. As Emily told us of her memories it awakened something in me, a glimmer of running with two people through a meadow, not my parents but...an old man and woman...something about their ability to call the animals to them. We were surrounded by birds, rabbits, squirrels and other small creatures. The memories were flashes, brief scene accompanied by feelings of euphoria.

Grandmother leaned close to me and asked, "You starting to remember, hmmm?"

I drew back and stared at her, amazed at the strange possibility that I had always known these two cherished friends.

Dorothy added to Emily's story. "Ever since she could talk she'd tell me about the Happy People. I always thought they were imaginary friends but I didn't discourage her. I went along with what, I thought then, was a game." Dorothy was a small woman in her thirties and dainty like her daughter. Her auburn hair and fair skin alleged Irish heritage.

Emily looked intently into her mother's face, her little hands reaching up to touch her cheek. "Remember when Daddy died and I told you that he was with the Happy People? That was true but you thought I was making it up, didn't you?"

Dorothy nodded, smiling, and asked, "Emily, will you tell our friends what happened the night of the accident?" She turned to us and explained, "This is what she told me when we were in the hospital."

The child was so natural and unaffected as she related that night's story. "Well," she began, leaning back into Grandmother's arms, "I knew I had died because I was with Daddy and Grandma but they told me that I had to go back because there was something very special I had to do on earth. Then I woke up and was on Walt's lap and I was so happy to see him again, in real life not just a dream. When we were riding in the ambulance with the lights on and the siren making noise I wasn't scared at all but Mama kept crying 'cause she thought I was hurt bad but later I told her all about what it was like and about Walt and Grandmother. I don't think she *really* believed me 'til that night in the hospital when Walt and Grandmother came to me and we all went to Mama's room. Was she surprised! She asked them if they were angels." Emily giggled and snuggled against Grandmother, who gathered the child to her.

She kissed Emily's cheek and said, "All over world people be seeing what they call angels. Angels be Light, like Walt and Grandmother, helping to show the way. Strange things happening now. You be hearing about this more and more. Light showing up in other ways too. People be seeing woman they call Mary. She appearing all over world too. This be female energy telling people to shape up."

I smiled at the image of Mary, solemnly appearing to the multitude who await her pious words: "Shape up!" I had always been inclined to disbelieve the Marion visions, thinking it was either propaganda of the Church or the product of delusional minds. I mean, *really*. I used to laugh and say that if I began a rumor that Mary was hanging out in my shed I could make a fortune on an unceasing parade of believers!

Jeff placed more wood on the fire as Grandmother continued speaking. "Female energy returning. People be finding the Goddess, the female side." She paused momentously as if the next words were waiting in the silence and once these words became sound a great shaking would occur like the reverberation felt as a plane breaks the sound barrier. "Old beliefs bubbling up again. Oh, yes, these ancient ways becoming known in women's nighttime exploration."

Grandmother had spoken to Dorothy's ancient Irish soul for her eyes held fascination as if she were homesick for the mysterious past. "Old ways?" Dorothy asked.

"Ohhh," Grandmother crooned and the wind sighed with her. "That be way of life when women reached through time," she answered. "Another name for these women be...Holy Women, Wiccans, Witches."

"Witches?" asked Robert, startled.

"Oh, not be what people think," she chuckled. "Wicca, Witch—she be woman in village who be healer, midwife, herbcrafter, wise woman who lives in rhythm with seasons. Word Witch was first 'wych' and that meant 'to bend, to shape.' This mean that Witch have power to bend or shape her life. She be very close to Light. In Native tribe she be called Medicine Woman, Shaman."

"Then why were we taught that a Witch is an evil, ugly old woman?" Shelly asked.

"Oh, that," she waved her hand in dismissal. "That be male energy there." She settled in, shifting positions with Emily in her arms, obviously very pleased with her audience around the circle, content that it was storytelling time. Her voice took on an awed timbre. "Many, many years ago and far, far away the village Witch be revered. Oh, yes, everybody go to her with problems, with questions. She know about healing, about birth, life, death even. Men then not scared of her power. They know it help whole village.

"Wicca lived by two codes: Harm None and Threefold Law. Threefold law be that whatever you do, positive or negative, come back to you three times stronger than it be sent out. Sooo, you send out good stuff you get back much good. You send out bad stuff, better watch out 'cause it come back like boomerang and knock you off feet!"

Then she sighed sadly. "But then people with different ways, different beliefs come and see these women and they be scared of her power. They say her power come from devil. Now, Witches, they be puzzled. They say, 'Hmmm, who be this devil fellow?' See, they not believe in devil. They not know about him, even. Well, bad times come then. They take Wicca woman away, torture her, try to make her confess she be working for devil. They try to make her give names of other women who be Witches." She shook her head and gazed into the flames. The mockingbird called from deep with the forest.

"They burn her in fire. Nine million people killed then, most be women. Those times now be known as 'Burning Times.' For long, long time people think there be no more Witches or Holy Women or that there never really be such women, that it all be superstition but they be around, all right, only they be in secret. Now they be coming out. Witches like to say they 'coming out of broom closet.'" She chuckled before continuing, "And they be coming out now 'cause world needs them to balance. Things began to balance again at time of your grandmothers. They be slow, slow hard changes. Women fight for vote, women get to have own property. Then about thirty years ago changes came faster and more and more."

Shelly spoke up. "That was the Women's Liberation Movement and the Equal Rights Amendment, right?"

Grandmother nodded. "That be right, Shelly. All changes come with hard struggles. Struggles still going on. Many men still not want to see woman-power. They be thinking it take something away from them. They not know about true power within. This be why there be so much violence to women but now," she lifted her hands and waved them around, "things moving fast like vortex, spinning topsy-turvy. Oh, boat gonna' be rockin' lots! This be time when all ancient beliefs be ready to come alive again. This be time to learn value of herbal ways, of vision quests, of moon planting, of living close, close to Mother Earth."

Can our tomorrows open to this vision of which Grandmother speaks? It sounded so wonderful as she spun her words around us. In my mind I saw the Village Wise Women, the Elders, the children, the men and the women planting gardens, learning the old ways of herbal cures, dancing country dances on village greens. I saw gentle, strong men loving gentle, strong women. I saw gay men and lesbians living who they are fearlessly, loving candidly, sharing their spirited selves. People of all colors, all races reached across borders to help each other navigate into those places that, for centuries, were forbidden. Children were surrounded by music, art, storytelling and were soothed with words of guidance, words of encouragement and comfort. I could almost feel that place, that time, those people.

Grandmother, like an artist painting our possible future upon the canvas of imagination, held her arms out to us as if by doing so she could pull us into her comfort. "You have gifts within you." Her clenched fist touched her chest and she frowned. "Gifts you say 'no' to every day. You walk through days of hell and you be blind that path to heaven be right under feet, at next step. Magic be in your mind and in your blood. Magic be life. See ways of science, ways of Wicca, blend them and *live* balance, *live* magic."

If I could live in Grandmother's mind, if I incorporated her visions into my spirit I would be able to release the chain of my body and fly in the night. Ohhh, I could stand at the silent center of the world and see the truths in old legends, the veracity of faery lore, the spellbinding power of words. Life seemed to vibrate with joy and mystery when seen through her eyes, when heard from her words. She handed me the Philosopher's Stone and urged me to fathom its worth, to see what brewed beneath its hard surface.

Ghostly spirals of smoke spun above the fire and the sounds of the night were amplified as katydids joined crickets in a midnight chorus. The full moon had risen, a golden globe above the treetops. This moon that had called humanity from the beginning, this moon that man had walked upon still spoke to us, still pulled the ocean's waters and communicated with females in their monthly cycle.

The drone of the night insects seemed to hush as Walt began to speak, his penetrating eyes sparkling in the fire's illumination. "This magic is waiting. It is life's gift. All around you," he gestured, "and within you is life, pure being. Human, animal, plant, soil, water, air—everything filled with life interrelating. In your finite minds try to imagine a Source so great as to be unnamable, and this Source, or energy, desires to experience...and so expands. What your scientists call the 'Big Bang' is when this energy *became*."

A sudden gust of wind pulled sparks from the fire, like bits of radiant rubies, and sent them dancing into the sky. The luscious smell of the woods, the campfire and the aromas of sandalwood, apples and cinnamon that always accompanied Grandmother wafted through the night air and seemed to settle into misty indigo shadows. Walt's velvet voice, like a secret language, unveiled the essence of life. "This moment, this natal pulse, was the primal energy creating itself, or the God/Goddess experiencing life through every star, every atom, every creature, every person. You have been taught that the Creator is everywhere and yet some feel it blasphemous to conclude that if this is truth then the Creator is in...*you*."

He paused. Time passed slowly, steeped in drifting moonlight, as we gazed at him, spellbound and mute. "Can it be possible," he asked, holding out his hands in question, "that a sperm and egg unite and spend nine months going through the mind-boggling process of creating organs, nerves, blood, bone, tissue and most amazing of all, a *brain,* then pushes its way through the birth canal to breathe its first breath, only so that it may grow to maturity, serve time in a job it hates, go home at night to eat and sleep? Can this person who came from invisibility into one cell, that cell dividing and each cell *knowing* if it should be brain cell, bone cell, eyes, ears or any of the millions of body parts...can it be that this person has nothing greater to do on earth than take up space, consume and then die? *What is it* within the DNA that holds the code to create such a miracle as you? For, my dear friends, you truly are that. You are *miracles*!"

George stretched his hands toward the fire and, his eyes moving from Walt to Grandmother, asked softly, "Why...?" His voice waver and he coughed. "Why is everything so hard for us? Why do so few of us act like we're miracles?" He leaned back, shifting to find a comfortable position for his old bones, his eyes sad.

Grandmother chuckled and answered, "Oh, it be like some old fairy tale. Once upon a time there lived great, noble king who had spell cast upon him. He leaves kingdom and all nice stuff and walks around thinking he be poor, silly old blockhead. That how it be with most people. They have all this good stuff inside, all this power, and they be walking through life like bumbling fools."

Walt agreed, then added, "You live your lives as ones asleep, in a dream. It's as though in entering this world you enter a theater of drama in which everyone agrees to pretend that whatever happens on the screen is real. You sit down in your seats and, depending upon what is shown upon the screen, you laugh, cry, scream, are inspired, become anxious, depressed. While the theater is darkened and you are focused only upon the screen it is very real to you. When the lights come on you may laugh at your own silliness in feeling all those emotions over things that are not real." He bent forward, resting his arms on his knees, then continued. "It is your task here to awaken, to see the Light so that you can know Who you truly are. God/Goddess is peeking out of *your* eyes."

Don scowled in thought. I was just beginning to know Don. He was very quiet and had seldom offered any information on his personal life but over these months I learned that he had been in jail for six months for drug possession and since his release five years ago had turned his life onto another path. He had used drugs for mind-expansion experience but then searched for drug-free means to reach heightened consciousness: meditation and yoga. He once told me, "Since I turned fourteen I've tried everything to keep from living what Thoreau called, 'a life of quiet desperation.' Oh, sometimes I was desperate...but it was never quiet. I did the drug scene, different religions and then I found a book on meditation and Eastern religion and that's when my real search began, when things began to make sense and I felt, finally, that my destiny was in my own hands. That's when I finally returned home and went into business with my brothers."

After considering Walt's words he nodded thoughtfully and said, "Our lives *are* like that, aren't they? A dream. How can we know what's dream and what's reality? I mean, while we're experiencing life we just don't know what else there is, we don't *know*..." he stopped, exasperated at his inability to put words to his thoughts.

Walt smiled in understanding. "It is through searching, through keeping your mind open to possibilities, through seeing life's wonder that you awaken. Some people's lives are not merely dreams, however, but nightmares and the pain those nightmares cause is real indeed to those involved. If you were thrashing and screaming in the grip of a nightmare would you not want to be awakened? If one were mentally disturbed and seeing threatening things crawling on the wall would they not want to be relieved of those illusions? As humanity evolves they will see the illusions. Do you imagine that humanity is a finished creature? Why...you've barely begun! At this time when most people use a minuscule measure of their power they see not the Light, they know not Who they are. What is unfamiliar you shut off and label supernatural."

I interrupted, "But Walt, you say humanity is *evolving* into this, then what about the Wise Women, the Shamans, all those ancients who knew things *so long ago*?"

"Ahhh," he answered, "they were the forerunners, the light-bearers, those few who were advanced far beyond the majority. Every evolvement begins with one who sees deeper, one who strays from the herd. Then another glimpses, and another. It takes many, many years for the majority to catch up."

The moon's light vanished behind swiftly gliding clouds. I thought about those who knew, the ones who dared to voice their insights. Why is it that humanity never welcomes this wisdom? Instead we kill the voice so that we can remain in our guarded ignorance. Shelly, sitting beside Walt, asked, "How do we encourage this evolvement? Is it something one is born to or can it be learned?"

Walt leaned back and looked into the darkness beyond the firelight, deep in thought before answering. "Both. Everyone has the potential, the seed, within him or her at birth. It is what one does with the seed, through mind, that decides if you walk with the majority or, as my Thoreau so aptly put it, 'march to a different drummer.' Mind, you see, is more than brain matter. Mind is...why, mind is..." he held out his arms to the sky, "God/Goddess. It is your *core*. It is within the very genetic instruction of your DNA.

"When mind seeks within nature and science, within the words of those who lived in the Light, mind comes to a place where it is vulnerable to the Light. When I speak of Light I speak not metaphorically but literally. All matter in its highest form is light. *You are Light*."

We are Light? Literally—Light, Walt is telling us. Tennyson spoke of this...this longing to know this light:

But what am I?
An infant crying in the night:
An infant crying for the light:
And with no language but a cry.

And Goethe knew:

Someday perhaps the inner light will shine forth from us,
and then we shall need no other light.

Why then? Why do we disbelieve that we are miracles and Light? Why do we believe we are nothing, a brief breath then gone?

Walt had seen deep into me and gave answer: "You must dig through life's trash, through the hackneyed, the dogma, the negative until the core of Light is discovered. This core is the substance of life, it is what all the seers, prophets and, yes, some scientists have seen. Life *is* the energy and light which is in all things. Nothing can exist but within it. If all matter is this Light and energy has it the hardness that you perceive? It has not.

"Therefore, all the power you have given matter does not exist. It is your agreed upon illusion. The teacher Jesus knew this, lived this, when he manipulated matter. He worked miracles, not to aggrandize his self but to show the illusion and he said, 'If you have faith you can do these things...and greater things.' Do you see that in this knowing, the hardness of cancer is dispersed, the hardness of blindness is dispersed, the hardness of anger and war and poverty would be known as agreed-upon illusions."

As time passed earth-scent grew rich and damp and a covering of dew began to settle upon us. I leaned closer to the fire and frowned, trying to grasp Walt's words. Part of me saw but part still clung to what my senses experienced in the "hardness."

Walt, smiling, spoke my name. "Diana, you seem disturbed. Do you not understand what I have spoken?"

"I'm confused," I answered, scowling. "You seem to be telling us that we can live as Jesus lived, that we can perform miracles, heal the sick, walk on water…"

He took a deep breath. "Ahhh, but you *can*."

"I can barely balance my checkbook! Walking on water is a bit beyond me."

"Oh, but of course it is. *If you say so.*"

I thought for a moment then realized what he meant. "If *I* say so." *Within, within*, a voice seemed to be insistently whispering.

After a moment he continued. "As we have told you, humanity is self-hypnotized. You live your beliefs. *You become your beliefs.* There is a longing within the heart of every person urging them to seek a higher life but too often this longing is not examined but followed blindly. If you do not know that heaven is *within you,* you will seek outside. This gnawing need propels my people: a mate might fulfill them, children might fulfill them, a new house, more and finer furniture, a closet bulging with the latest fashions, a more beautiful body and face, a job with more status and money, a fatter bank account, a wilder social life and, in recent years, the easy high of drugs…that escape from emptiness. You are led to believe that happiness lies at the end of a checkout counter. If any of these things had the power of lasting fulfillment why is it that the recipients of any or all of them aren't necessarily happy and are often miserable? You have hypnotized yourselves into slavery, into lives of desperation and spiritual poverty and alienation. Oh, my people, it is time to *awaken*!"

After an interval of silence in which we grappled with these teachings, Jeff hesitantly questioned, "But desires…aren't they in us for a reason? Are you telling us we shouldn't enjoy things, desire things?"

Wraithlike coils of fog rose up from the forest floor and seemed to dance in the distance as clouds drifted over the light of the waxing moon. Walt answered, "Recall the words just spoken: 'There is a longing within the heart of every person urging them to seek a higher life. But too often this longing is not examined but followed blindly.' It is the *unexamined* desires that can lead to sorrow and a feeling of emptiness. Life and living are sacred. Enjoy! *But enjoy in wisdom!*"

As his words ended all was silent, save for the sounds from the forest and the crackling fire. Emily was asleep in her mother's arms and Jake, who had wandered down the path to our campsite, contentedly drowsed on Robert's lap while we thought and waited. Finally George spoke. "What are we supposed to do with all you're teaching us?"

Everyone seemed to lean forward in anticipation. *What is expected of us? What is our future?* Grandmother stirred, her dark eyes moving to each of us. "When one walks Mystery Path one be changed forever. It not be what *we* expect of you but what *you* expect from selves."

Jeff asked, "We don't have to try to change other people?"

Grandmother's brows drew together. "*Never*," she said emphatically. "How can you know what path be best for them to follow?"

"But you've said that the Light is touching the world and it will go from person to person," Jeff insisted.

Grandmother nodded, "That be right. Light touch people, not you. This be where big mistake be made all through time. Oh," she sighed, "so much pain caused by people who think they have one true answer for everybody. When enough people live in Light then world start to change."

I was so relieved to hear this I audibly groaned and whispered, "That's a relief!"

Grandmother turned to me and inquired, "You think this be easy, hmmm? You think walking own path in Light be big picnic, no troubles, no problems? Ohhhh, you on tough path, Diana. This be hardest path in life."

"What do you mean?" I asked cautiously. Do I want to hear this my inner voice warned?

She looked at me, into me, her obsidian eyes filled with compassion. "Diana, we give you lessons now to help in days to come. Everyone must listen carefully." She turned to the others in the fire circle. "We not be coming to you just for good time by firelight. We here to help you open own powers, to be strong, be wise. People of Mother Earth being given chance to make choice. Things so out of balance it be like you teetering on edge of cliff. You be on journey to learn how to balance." As she spoke she lifted her flute but before putting her lips to it she softly said, "Be kind to Mother Earth. Be kind to selves, to each other." The silver flute in her small hands caught the fire's light and seemed to move like a living thing. "Ohhh, you be more wonderful than ever you imagine."

As her words echoed she put her silver flute to her lips, breathed life into it and the notes circled us and sparkled upon us. The firelight and creatures within the deep woods kept rhythm with her. "Listen!" they chorused.

The grove seemed to come alive as each tree, every bush, the forest floor itself pulsated with the vital energy of God/Goddess. My eyes closed, unable to cope with the myriad colors and sounds enveloping us. How can we, dwarfed in our observance of life, blind to all but that which is survival, open our eyes to Creation?

The otherworldly timelessness softened and loosened and as I became aware of my surroundings I opened my eyes and, just as I had feared, our two teachers were gone. As always, in the moments after they departed, I experienced a loneliness. Even surrounded by all these friends I felt that a part of myself had vanished.

Chapter 7

Between the Worlds

Our eyes begin to open. The eye sealed behind our skulls stirs from its slumber but what is revealed in the dawning Light, so foreign to fledglings, often causes us to desire nothing more than to return to the darkness of ignorance. We journey to the edge, where the veil is thin, where the moon hangs low in the night sky, where the cosmos is a shapeshifter.

Spirals within spirals, circles within circles, the Wheel of Life resonates in magic as the two threads, wave and particle, weave the tapestry of the universe. Within the inhalation and exhalation of life there are many points of power, many times of choice.

Summer, so welcomed in New England with its seemingly endless days of ocean's surf, foghorns moaning on mist-shrouded nights, sun-filled forests in which one can wander for hours, clam bakes and barbecues, fishing boats and sunburned tourists had eased into that startling day when the first autumn leaf was spotted carrying with it a certain sadness. The first crimson leaf was a presage of the frozen days to come. My summer euphoria always gave me the delusion that autumn was far in the future.

September filled my gardens with marigolds, asters, cosmos, dahlias, zinnias and chrysanthemums. Morning glories fell on either side of my front door like a waterfall of blue and green and recent rainfalls returned the emerald grass which had faded to straw in the months of scant rain. The morning opened clear and blue-skied, sunlight brilliant against the long shadows of dawn and the soft breeze carried the scent of marigolds and apples. The symphony of dawn played and I lifted my face to the sky where a V of Canada geese listened to autumn's warning. As my eyes followed the geese over the treetops I noticed that the light had changed. The soft spring light had become the golden yellow light of summer and now it was transformed into a deep, fiery glow that seemed to celebrate the inevitable change of seasons.

As was my routine on Saturday mornings, I sat at the picnic table despite the chill, drank my coffee and wrote in my journal, continuing my strange tale. I had seen Walt and Grandmother only once since our Midsummer ceremony. Shelly and I had been wandering through the meadow at The Cliffs when Grandmother's flute called us. Instead of our long hours with our teachers they had made an appearance only to encourage us because Leonard's harassment had increased. He seemed the only flaw in my life but one I found impossible to dismiss. His Biblical threats continued to appear on our doors, the windshield of my car had been smashed and the most threatening and frightening was what he had done to my poor kitty Jake.

Jake had been missing for two days and I was frantic for he was not one to stray too far and miss out on meals. Late one night I heard crying and found him crouched in the cedar grove with strings of tin cans tied to his back legs. His long, orange fur was matted, his eyes were wild and, once I had gotten him inside and cut the strings from his legs I saw they were cut and swollen where the string had dug into them. He limped to his dish where, barely able to stand, he drank his water dish dry. After the veterinarian had treated him I took the receipt, in a rage, to the police station and again reported Leonard's torment and, once again, was told there was no proof it was Leonard nor was there even any way to identify who this person was but I had no doubts at all that Leonard was carrying out his threat that he would stop us, using Jake as a warning.

They did, however, take me seriously for Robert also reported that his beautiful gardens had been trashed, wilted flowers strewn across his lawn. Jeff had been aghast to find a cross with a lightening bolt upon it painted on the hood of his car and being a black man, took the threat of a cross gravely, as did the police. Leonard, crafty creep that he was, had discontinued following us in his car because that would give us his plate number and, of course, his identity. All the law could do was watch our homes and try to find someone fitting his description.

After Jake's disappearance and injury I no longer allowed my cats to go outside alone and they demonstrated their outrage by scratching at the doors and howling on the window sills. I felt empathy for them because I also felt like a prisoner in my home, afraid to leave, afraid to sleep, outraged that this maniac could cause me to feel such fear. A man monstrous enough to injure Jake, so trusting and affectionate, may not stop there. Leonard was one who felt he was on God's mission, therefore able to use any means necessary to destroy those whom he felt were evil and in his distorted mind anyone who did not adhere to his crazed beliefs was evil. No wonder Walt and Grandmother were so adamant about us not trying to change anyone's life or belief—this is what it could lead to. The last time I saw her Grandmother reminded me of the law of the Wise Woman, "Do what you will and harm none" but she gave no instruction on how to *stop* Leonard in his madness. Both she and Walt repeated what they'd told us before, to focus and center. I recalled Walt's awesome words spoken to us while at the bridge: "When you get to the point in your growth when you know that you are God you will be incapable of feeling fear."

Oh, I wished that they were there with me. That statement itself seemed a sort of madness. Isn't that what crazed people assumed? That they were God, or Godlike? Where is the fine line between knowing your own sanctity and deluding yourself that you are above others and therefore can act in accordance and trample over their beliefs? When was the cold and dark moment Hitler stepped over that line and entered a shadowy realm where his mind conceived of gas chambers and the holocaust of millions?

It was all so confusing, this Journey, as Grandmother called it. I sipped my cold coffee as I closed the notebook and pushed it aside, staring into space. Walking back to the house my mind continued to struggle with the answers: how to end the fear, how to stop the feelings of victimization, how to end Leonard's cruelty without harming him, as the law of the Wise Woman instructed. Most puzzling of all, how to know you are God without going mad. Ahhh, for the days of peaceful ignorance.

I felt a stab of anger as I unlocked my back door, provoked by the feeling that I felt so unsafe that I couldn't walk into my back yard without securing my home against *him.* My pleasure of awakening to such a peaceful morning was shattered now and, as I prepared to leave to have breakfast with my two children at the coffee shop, I worked to regain it. Both my children were sensitive to my moods and I wanted to give them no cause to ask questions I couldn't answer. I had told them about the new people I had met but Walt and Grandmother was a subject I didn't care to open to them. Anyone who hadn't experience what I and the others had would think I was as mad as the proverbial Hatter. Even when they are adults children expect a certain stability from their parents. Mark and Katrina would not take it well if I told them of Mother's New Friends. In fact, I strongly believe that they would put their two heads together and quietly discuss putting M-o-m in the H-o-m-e. They view me as somewhat eccentric but harmless, never one to stray into forbidden zones where heavenly entities lurked. I doubt that it would ever enter their imaginations that Mom and her pals chanted in the forest with Really Big Celebrities or that she was being stalked by Leonard the Depraved. I could be wrong. Maybe someday I could find a way to tell them, something sane and subtle. I doubt they would take it well if I did anything too theatrical. I shouldn't, for instance, levitate into the heavens or make a display of myself by *glowing* in public.

Later, after breakfast and errands, I returned home and spent the afternoon raking leaves which were beginning to fall from autumn's trees. I think I rake leaves more for the fun of it than to clean the yard. Huge piles of wonderfully aromatic leaves that rustle and blow in the wind like flying bouquets. Huge piles of leaves that cats adore tunneling into then suddenly jumping out of, startled and wild, chasing each other in delicious games.

When I unlocked my front door, wind-blown and happy, the phone was ringing and I stumbled over cats on my way to answer it. Shelly's voice on the other end asked, "Diana, what do you think of planning a wonderful Halloween celebration this year? We could invite everyone and have some sort of ceremony. I've done some research on the old ways of Halloween. Do you know it was called Samhain? I think it would be fitting to honor the change of seasons."

I caught her enthusiasm and invited her over for supper and for planning this great event. I made fresh pesto sauce from the remaining basil in my garden and an apple cobbler with apples from my one fruit tree then worked in the studio until Shelly arrived. The scent of the spiced apples was still fragrant in my home and Shelly commented, "Your house always smells so old-fashion—wood smoke, good cooking. Yum."

I brewed two cups of a wonderful blend of coffee beans I had bought that morning in a local health food store and we walked outside with our steaming cups as the sun was beginning to set. The darkening came so early now. When the shortened days first begin I feel somehow cheated, but once accepted it's kind of cozy to just settle in at the end of the day by a wood fire.

The wind blew and Bess, Jake and Cricket returned to their game with renewed enthusiasm, scrambling about with maddened eyes, ears back, leaping to bring down those elusive leaves, managing a few tricky spins even Nijinsky would envy. These cats were Olympic material. We sat at the picnic table, wrapped in our jackets and holding our cups to warm our hands silently watching as sunlight sank into the trees beyond the meadow. Lingering rays cast themselves over the tips of grasses like a field of jewels.

"Ahhh," Shelly sighed, as the scene before us faded into dusk, "what a show. Thanks for inviting me over. I wouldn't have wanted to miss that."

"It's renewing, isn't it?" I asked. "Watching nature, being a part of it puts life in perspective."

She nodded. "Sometimes I get so caught up in life-stuff: work, house, car, bills, repairs, all the worries, bla, bla, bla. Then I begin to feel dry, life gets kind of gray. I don't even realize what's missing I'm so involved. Then I see something like that and—whoosh! It's like a blanket of peace wraps around me and clears my eyes."

Darkness caused us to leave the starlit autumnal evening and return to the house, the lights through the windows welcoming us like beacons. I called the cats and they bolted inside, famished after play. The scents of cooking made me realize how hungry I'd become and we began to prepare supper. While we waited for the pasta water to boil we set the table, made a salad and chatted about the upcoming festivities.

"So, tell me about this research on Halloween that you did," I said.

She walked to where her purse was on the countertop, came back with a paperback book and held it up for me to see. The title read, "Under The Moon: A Reflection of the Wonders of Witchcraft." I wiped my hands on a towel and reached for it, flipping through its pages and reading the page of contents. "This looks really interesting. Where did you get it?" I asked as I studied the mystical nocturnal scene on its front cover.

"Well," she began, her face alight with excitement, "first I went to the local library and they didn't have much so I went into the Boston Library where there was a huge section on Witchcraft and New Age religions. I spent hours there! Then I found a bookstore in Harvard Square called, 'The Closet.' I bought this book and several others, some crystals, a pentacle ring..." She held up her hand for my inspection and I admired a beautiful ring with a silver circle in which was a star formed of triangles, a tiny turquoise stone set in its center.

"What are you getting into? Witchcraft?" I laughed as I shook pasta from its package into the boiling water.

"It's all the stuff Grandmother talked about! Remember? Grandmother said it was ancient, and good and whole. That's what I feel about it. There is nothing evil at all here. It just feels right and you don't have to join any church or have a leader. You can be solitary in these beliefs."

While we enjoyed our meal together she read parts of the book to me. "What I like about this is that it blends science and mysticism. The author talks about quantum physics, the nature of light and matter and how the Holy Women instinctively knew all this stuff that science is now teaching. How did they know, for instance, about the mind-body connection that doctors are just beginning to recognize?

How did they know about space-time and the unity of all things and particles, waves and energy? They knew, long before there were microscopes or telescopes, the nature of the universe and our place in it. How?"

She lifted her eyes from the page and said eagerly, "Don't you see, Diana? In all these books I'm reading is everything Walt and Grandmother have been teaching us. They teach a love and reverence for Mother Earth, the power of the female, the balancing, the magic of the universe."

"Much like the Native American and the Eastern beliefs," I mused.

"All this ties in with what we experience with Walt and Grandmother. I can't prove how it happened or why us or why now but it's a kind of magic that we create."

"Are you saying that it's all in our minds, a fantasy we're conjuring?"

She shook her head emphatically and answered, "Not at all! When you read about quantum physics you begin to understand. One of the physicists, Niels Bohr, said, 'Anyone who isn't shocked by quantum physics doesn't understand it.' She put the book aside and asked, "Do you see? Nothing is how we were taught! We create by *participating* and what we create is *real*."

I shook my head and murmured, "It's hard to grasp, isn't it? I've given up trying to make any sense, any logic, out of Walt and Grandmother."

"But it *does* make sense, according to quantum physics! I can't really explain it all. I can barely grasp it myself with the edge of my poor brain. When I read the books I begin to understand but I can't really explain it to anyone else yet. I know that while I'm reading I understand how we have these experiences with Walt and Grandmother. This is why I'm so excited about creating a ceremony on

Halloween night, or Samhain, as the ancients called it. I feel a need to *knowingly* participate in something very old and very wise. When we held our Midsummer ceremony I went into it blindly and my confusion didn't allow me to forget myself and just be a part of it."

I agreed that I, too, had gone into that night as more entertainment and camaraderie than for a deeply spiritual experience. "Do you have any ideas of what you'd like to do?" I asked.

She lay her fork down, wiped her mouth on her napkin then leaned back in the chair. "Magic," she said matter-of-factly.

"You really believe in magic?" I asked, nodding toward the book that lay on the table.

She stared at me, amazed. "How can you feel that way after what we've seen? It's not hocus-pocus or trickery."

"A certain amount of skepticism is healthy," I answered. "What you said before about blending science and mysticism, that's what I'm needing. I need to know more about the science part of magic before I can participate. Otherwise I'll feel it was all superstitious nonsense."

The rich aroma of the coffee brewing surrounded us as I poured two big mugs and carried them to the table. "Before you can participate?" Shelly laughed skeptically. "What do you think you've been doing these past months?"

I was silent as I stirred honey into my coffee and pondered what she'd suggested. Magic? Witchcraft? Is that what this has been about?

She seemed to read my thoughts when she said, "Does it need a label? Magic, Witchcraft—just words. You can just as easily call it quantum physics, theology, philosophy."

I lit candles around the living room and we curled up in big chairs by the warm fire, sipping our coffee, enjoying the apple cobbler and sharing stories and mysteries long into the night.

`Autumn was unusually warm that year and my gardens continued to bloom untouched by frost. Even the tender dahlias thrived, their vibrant shades of pink, red, yellow and russet nodding under the gentle breeze. Huge sluggish bumblebees droned over the last drops of summer's nectar. I smiled as I snipped stems, piling the huge blossoms onto one arm, silently thanking the Source that gave such beauty. These bouquets were placed around my home along with pumpkins carved into scary faces to illuminate this Halloween, or Samhain evening. The front steps displayed several potted mums and two huge carved pumpkins ready to greet the wandering children asking for treats.

I knew from my recent research with Shelly that Samhain was known in the old earth religions, to the Witches, as the night of the New Year, the night when the veil between the two worlds was very thin: the world of matter and spirit, the world of the living and those who've traveled beyond this realm. It was a night of mystery, of possibilities, of receiving wisdom from beyond. It was a night when we might be reunited with Walt and Grandmother.

As the afternoon deepened and the day's warmth was pushed aside by the coming night's chill, I placed logs and kindling in the glass-front wood stove, touched a match to them and waited as the newspaper caught, then the kindling and soon the flames were tasting the logs and I could feel the heat from the stove's blowers as I adjusted the damper. After the candles inside the pumpkins were lit and the fierce faces glared around the room I switched on the front light and lit the jack-o-lanterns on the steps. As I prepared for the arrival of ghosts, pirates, and whatever specter was currently popular I thought back to my own feelings of being a child on Halloween night. Back then no one even conceived of danger to children as we were driven by parents into the center of town where we were free to roam the neighborhood without adults—a delicious sensation. Oh, the wonder of being unrecognized behind a costume, of walking through the windy night kicking up leaves, approaching a house where anything might answer the knock—even a Witch! Such exhilaration was experienced when, home at last and safe, I would open the bag for the audit of the booty! Do children still feel the mystery of this night?

The first knock sounded on the door just as I was pouring the contents of three bags of candy into a basket and when I unlocked the door the ritual 'Trick or Treat' greeted me. The night brought an array of all manner of creatures seeking that life-sustaining elixir —sugar. By nine o' clock the cavalcade of the weird had waned and I muttered as I eyed the lone candy bar at the bottom of the basket, "Little creeps never leave me any," making a vow that next year I would buy enough candy to enable me to make myself pleasantly ill.

I locked the storm door, leaving the main door open so I could see when my next guests arrived. Throughout this night of opening the door to strangers I'd felt an uneasiness, anticipating a visit from Leonard. Now *that* was scary! As I was preparing a fresh pot of coffee and a snack the knock came and I peeked into the living room seeing with relief George's sweet old face smiling through the glass.

"Hi, George," I smiled, opening the door.

"I'm not George. I'm Don wearing an old man mask," he chortled.

Smiling, I took the bundle George handed to me and we walked into the kitchen where he helped himself to a cup of decaf coffee. Immediately, we heard a chorus of familiar laughing voices yelling the night's demand, 'Trick or Treat' and when I opened the door my friends entered, filling the kitchen with their voices and laughter.

As I hugged Dorothy I asked, "Where's Emily? I was looking forward to seeing her."

Oh," she answered as she shrugged out of her jacket, "she was exhausted after she coaxed me into walking to every house in the neighborhood. My Mom stayed over and was putting her to bed as I was leaving."

Jeff draped his arm around my shoulders and handed me a bottle of wine, turning the label so I'd notice it. "Flying Witch Wine" it read, above a silhouette of a witch on a broom.

I burst out laughing. "Where did you get this?"

"An interesting little town in the Berkshires," he answered, smiling smugly. "Do you think it'll make us fly?"

"It will me!" I admitted. "One glass of wine and my fingertips get numb. Cheap date."

Shelly nudged him and asked with a smile, "Why did someone in this little town sell a wine called Flying Witch?"

He, Don and Robert exchanged a glance and I insisted, "What are you guys up to?"

"What's goin' on?" George asked, looking from one to another.

Jeff straddled a chair by the table, sipped his coffee, then said, "We went to the Berkshire Mountains with Grandmother."

"No!" I gasped. "When? Why just you guys? What happened?"

He held up his hand to ward off my questions and, chuckling, answered, "I think she felt we needed a big dose of seeing female power."

"Why wasn't I invited?" George pouted.

"We asked her that, George. She said, 'Oh, he be at advanced age when man hormones don't block brain stuff.'" Laughter exploded and George smiled, content that he wasn't in disfavor with Grandmother.

"So, what happened?" Shelly asked impatiently.

The three men explained that Grandmother had met them on a path while they were hiking one morning and insisted they drive her to the Berkshires. On the drive she explained about the balance that must come between male and female and of the powerful movement in the Berkshire Mountains of a return to the old earth religion in which Mother Earth is seen for what she is—the ancient female creative force. Without this balance in life we will continue to pollute, destroy, cause the extinction of animal species, spread racial hatred and intolerance, annihilate entire cultures and, finally, be the cause of the extinction of our own species.

Grandmother was not overtly noticed by the general population in the tiny town, a town accustomed to seeing Witches strolling along the old cobbled streets, black capes flowing. But the Witches, the women in black, these women smiled warmly at Grandmother, calling out greetings to her as if they knew her or shared a psychic bond.

The sunny afternoon found them high on a grassy hill where many women gathered, some in their black robes, others in ordinary clothing. A few men were scattered throughout the crowd but they had a quality about them that Jeff, Robert and Don found different from many men. They were not at all feminine yet there was something, a quiet, regal strength, a gentle knowing very much like Walt.

Finally, everyone settled down upon the grass and Grandmother stepped into the circle along with a young woman named Angelica. They spoke of the upcoming new year, Samhain, and its meaning and importance. Angelica's robes blew in the wind, her long, black curls escaping from under her hood. In relating this story to us Jeff said, "It was great. As I watched and listened I felt like I was witnessing something *so important*, that I was a part of a great change on earth."

By the time the men were finished telling us of their remarkable afternoon we had moved from the kitchen into the living room and were all seated around the cozy fire, cups of coffee and cocoa in our hands, trays of munchies on the coffee table.

We turned to Robert, his round wire-rimmed glasses reflecting the flames of the fire, as he continued the story. "These women were a wonder." He paused, his fist knotted in frustration as he strained for the right words to convey his emotions. "They touched me, reached me. I finally understood what the female is."

His fist touched his chest and he continued, "Our society, most societies, have given such a distorted picture of what women are—from playthings, to housewives, to whores, sometimes saintly martyrs. As men, we've been taught not to take women too seriously. We were *fed this* from day one! It was a subliminal message from everywhere—*men are better*. I didn't think I felt that way. I mean, I always felt I was somehow more enlightened than most men. Even as a kid I really liked females, always respected them but up on that hill, surrounded by all those wonderful, strong women, *I knew*. I knew that in the past, deep down I, too, had felt superior, if just a little bit."

"Don't you see where it all comes from?" Jeff asked, looking around the room at everyone. "God, we are taught, is male. Jesus is male, the apostles were male, Buddha, Gandhi, every one of any importance is male. There are only a few references to women in the Bible and most are negative. Even Mary is made sexless and somehow different from all other women. Throughout recorded history women are negated, ridiculed, despised."

Shelly spoke up, "Yes, *recorded* history and who recorded history? Men, but before that many societies were matriarchal and this is now being discovered by archeological digs."

"Women are stronger. That's a fact," George said. "Living with my wife all those years I came to see this."

"But, George," I interrupted, "that's what Grandmother and Walt tell us we have to get away from—who's stronger, who's better. We have to stop this division and try to balance each other. It's the *balance* they keep stressing. If we start doing to men what's been done to us we'll be no better off. We have to start creating partnerships, valuing each others' strengths, helping each other in our weaknesses rather than take advantage of those weaknesses to gratify our egos."

The discussion was energetic and it occurred to me that perhaps this was a distinct moment in time, a split from the years of abuse and violence, that unknowingly we had taken a new path into a new world. Who can know, while it begins, that a crack has begun? Who saw, who heard the resounding split in the universe when the first person used fire at her hearth?

Dorothy set her cup carefully on the coffee table and stood, asking, "Do you have anything planned for tonight?"

I shook my head and answered, "You and I have talked about this but we didn't really decide any sort of ceremony. We all know now what this night means. What do you think?" I asked, searching their faces.

Dorothy reached for her jacket where it lay on the sofa and said, "All night I've been wanting to return to that place in the woods where we were before." She motioned for us to remain seated and added, "If you want to stay here cozy by the fire that's okay. This is just something I'd like to do. Do you have a flashlight?"

Everyone got up and put on their jackets. "Lead on Dorothy."

George laughed, "Yeah, follow the yellow brick road."

Like children, we giggled and sang, "...follow the yellow brick road, follow the yellow brick road..." as we headed for the front door. I checked that all cats were inside before I locked the door and rushed off through the rustle of leaves, following the yellow beam of light, following the night's mystery.

We formed a single line into the forest, our steps crunching the fallen leaves, the cry of a lone crow announcing his surprise at our intrusion. When we came to the open circle I saw that the fire stones were as we'd left them at Midsummer and the wind chimes still hung from the trees, singing their wind-song. Faded remains of ribbons flapped like tiny, wild spirits as we gathered fallen branches and broke them into kindling. Once the fire was blazing we stood around warming our hands by it, staring into the flames, listening, listening.

It came, softly, barely audible at first, possibly just the wind through the pines but I knew they were coming. A rose-haze mist shimmered as if coming from the flames, flute-song danced in silver filaments within the mist. The notes seemed to create form as Grandmother and Walt appeared, at first merely a faint outline as a drift of smoke but then deepening, more substantial until they stood by the fire before us with outstretched arms, ready to embrace us.

Our circle was complete as we sat in silent expectation with our teachers. Grandmother began. "This be night," she paused, gazing at each of us with her wise, ebony eyes, "of great mystery. You know this now, hmmm? You be learning without Grandmother and Walt? This be right way. Good teachers tell many things but they not *make* students think, search. We come to you to tell you great mysteries but you must take words, go back into world and learn more, grow more.

"Robert, Jeff and Don tell you about our day together. Shelly, Diana, Dorothy and George be learning from books. Dorothy be learning from Emily, even. Tonight we walk through veil, you learn from ancestor, Wise Woman from before Burning Times."

Her face in the firelight was rich in color, rich in wrinkles. She took Walt's hand in hers and they smiled into each others' eyes, a silent communication of old friends. Walt's long, gray hair and beard glistened like snow in moonlight. As he began speaking even the rustling of the trees ceased, as if listening to his poet's tongue. "Whitman once wrote, 'To me every hour of the light and dark is a miracle, every cubic inch of space is a miracle.' This is the foundation of the Craft of the Wise. Everything is spirit, everything is sacred. You can believe this or not. You can see this or not. If you believe this you *will* see, you will create *magic*.

"You are thinking, 'Is this magic real?' Yes, it is as real as the wind, as the forces of gravity and electricity. It is as real as you make it. Tonight...you will see. You will slip between time, between the ticks of the clock."

Grandmother and Walt rose gracefully from the ground, we stood with them and everyone held hands in a circle around the fire. She removed her flute from the leather case, which hung from her waist and holding it up like a silver wand she began spiraling on one foot while chanting. She called out to the four directions and continued to slowly turn clockwise and from the end of the flute a neon blue light appeared, growing more and more brilliant until the light, like a shimmering comet's streak, encircled us.

Breathless, we waited. The combined scents of apples, sandalwood, cinnamon and frankincense were heavy in the air and as the blue light luminescence radiated, a form began to emerge. A woman stepped from the blue light as one stepping through a doorway. I gasped. This was the woman we had seen so long ago at the coffee shop when Walt showed us the many faces of Creation. She was a dark woman of the forest, a wild thing that civilization could never own.

She raised her arms above her head, the wide sleeves of her black robe falling back and, like the night of the vision, upon her forehead, between her eyebrows was that strange blue tattoo. Setting on her raven hair was the silver band on which was centered two silver half-moons, the waxing and the waning, on either side of a full moon. I was stunned. The blue light faded, barely discernible. She lowered her arms and, gathering her black robes around her, sat on the ground between Walt and Grandmother. "My greetings to you." Her voice was husky, deep and rich as thick honey and I was stirred as if her voice flowed in my veins. "I am known by many names. I am your wisdom. On this night call me Viviane, She who lives."

On this night and where in plastic time is "this night?" How can it be that these things are happening to us, to me? Is reality so pliant that time and space can blur? Is there no distinction between spirit and matter? Do these profound things come into view from a parallel universe of the quantum world? Do we exist in a collection of possibilities?

Knowing my thoughts she spoke to me. "These things are truth...and more." Her burnished eyes seemed to smile as she spoke. It was easy to imagine her in a distant time walking across a heather-strewn meadow, her robes flying in the wind, a basket hooked over an arm as she searched for healing herbs in secret places. "The universe has many dimensions." She drew her gaze from me and her eyes swept the circle to include the others. Her voice seemed to drift in from the shadows of the trees. "You live in only four dimensions but all others are within those four, although in your daily lives you are not aware of them." Her voice seemed to rise up from the earth. "I was called from a field of dimension in which matter acts more like a wave than a particle, or more like spirit than matter." Her voice seemed to be carried to us from the beams of the moon. "This field is both past and future, as you have conceived time, and is in superposition—that is, two states of being at once."

I strained to hear and to understand for these words were new and strange. "The blue light you see is an observer-created reality which Grandmother's consciousness called forth. Your physicists would, in theory, call this a paradigm shift, a fundamental change in the patterns of that which shapes your reality. The light is the field of energy that shapes your world and is brought into visibility through superluminal participation."

She paused and I noticed the puzzled looks on the faces of my friends and from this I gained comfort that I wasn't alone in my feeble-mindedness. Viviane smiled in understanding and said, "I know you feel this is all beyond your comprehension but you will come to understand. Your scientists are beginning to glimpse these truths, certainties within which the ancients *lived*, knowing the interdependence of all life, the invisible world of the atom, the nonlocality of matter and that all events are driven by probabilities. Walt has spoken of your next evolution and it is this—you are to retrieve the wisdom of the ancients and carry it into the technology of this day. Only in this can your planet survive, only in knowledge of the interconnectedness of the universe will you finally live in peace."

Above us the crescent moon shone through the trees' swaying branches and all was silent except for the crackling fire. From this silence came the crashing of feet on the forest floor. My breath caught as I quickly looked around, trying to see, in the darkness, where the intruder was.

The blue light, faded to a hazy mist, hissed and snapped like firecrackers and Viviane was gone. My heart pounded as the sound grew louder and I heard the terrible words, "*Thou shalt not suffer a witch to live!*"

He strode into the light, fists clenched, face contorted in rage. "Sorcery! Wickedness!" he thundered.

He seemed to have grown taller, deadlier, and his eyes, though deeper in their storm, were clearer and more focused. A thunderbolt realization hit me with a shock. We were feeding him! Our fear, like blood to the mythical vampire, was allowing him to grow stronger, more confident. When we make an enemy we then fear them and it is this fear that is the forerunner of conflict, war, bloodshed.

He slowly walked toward us, a billowing dark aura followed him. When he spoke his voice was hard with hatred. "So...all of you together. Witches around the fire conjuring demons." He squinted and smirked.

Then he leaned forward toward us, reminding me of a maddened animal ready to attack. "God has chosen *me*! He has spoken in my ear." He looked piercingly at us. "Oh, I know what you think. I know." His voice shook. "You don't believe the Lord chose me. So filled with evil you can't see the Lord's messenger. Jeesusss came to me and He told me to destroy you like a nest of vipers."

It happened as if in slow motion. He reached into his jacket, drew out a gun and, taking two steps stood close to Walt, lifted the firearm and pointed it at Walt's head.

"Nooooooo!!" My scream resonated with the explosion that seemed to echo through eternity. I threw my head back and screamed, my eyes shut tight, not able to face my beautiful Walt. I was numb, unable to move and although this had happened in a second in time I felt caught in timelessness. The echo faded, replaced by the urgent cries of the crows.

I bent double with grief, clutching myself, a choking sob escaped my throat and then I heard his voice coming softly from the depths of sorrow. "Leonard. Ohhh, Leonard."

I opened my eyes and witnessed the miracle. Walt, unhurt, was gazing intently into Leonard's eyes. When Leonard had bent over to aim the gun at Walt the cross he wore around his neck had swung forward. Walt's hand had come up and firmly grasped it. He looked at the cross then into Leonard's eyes again.

"The one associated with this cross came with a message of love. Why then is your heart hardened against that message?"

Leonard tried to push his hand away, to stand straight but he was unable to move, was locked within Walt's steady gaze. He gritted his teeth and hissed, "I have given my *life* to Jesus!"

"He would not ask for you life but only that you value all life and see the miracle." The light within Walt seemed to be stroking the walls of Leonard's darkness as his slow deep voice caressed the stoniness.

"Satan! That's why you're not dead! Satan! Let...me...*go!*" He twisted his head and tried to draw back.

"Satan is an invention of those who would not see themselves. It is love we've come to give. Leonard...do you love?" Walt's voice was strong and steady, yet gentle.

He released the cross and Leonard sank to his knees, his head upon the ground. We held our breath at this scene before us, knowing not to interfere. *Something momentous was happening.*

From where he was kneeling, face hidden upon the earth, he groaned as if in agony, then raised his face to Walt. Through gritted teeth he spat, "I love God. You won't take that from me you evil..."

Walt reached down to touch him and he twisted away, his eyes rolling. "No!" He scurried on hands and knees out of Walt's reach. My gentle Walt remained tranquil. It appeared that he were part of the earth he sat upon. "Leonard, from the moment of your birth I have been with you."

Leonard placed his hands over his ears and shook his head from side to side as Walt continued. "I whispered to you on your arrival to earth. I welcomed you and told you of your astonishing worth. I spoke of the great tasks that lie ahead of you, of pain to be overcome, lessons to be learned. You came here to learn of love but have succeeded in learning only hate."

"You don't understand," he shouted. "You don't know what it was like!"

"Don't I? Your father drank, he beat you, he beat your mother and he walked out and left you when you were but eight years old. You often didn't have enough to eat. Your mother took her own life a year later and you were put in foster care where abuse continued." Walt's words were like a moving canvas for as he spoke them they seemed to paint themselves into pictures in our minds. "I know,

Leonard."

Leonard lay upon the ground as dread took hold of him. He twisted and moaned, "Shut up! Shut up!"

"You felt responsible for your mother's death, felt you should have been able to take care of her but, Leonard, you were so little yourself. As you grew your guilt and anger grew."

"Yes," Leonard howled, "my anger grew. If you know so much you'd know…"

"Ahh, but I do." Walt nodded his head. "The life my people often choose to lead is agonizing, especially to children. I cannot stop humanity's folly for that is their freedom."

Leonard whispered, "I have found *Jesus* and that has helped me to be righteous."

"Righteous?" Walt questioned. "You have not found Jesus. He was never missing. You have never lived his teachings. When you became an adult you were responsible to break the legacy your parents handed you. You had a choice."

"I did choose. I chose religion." He groaned deep in his throat, frustration building.

"Religion without love is dangerous. Do you love?"

Leonard remained on the ground, face-down in the dirt. His hands grasped his head as if he could shut out Walt's probing voice. Then, suddenly, he sat up, spun around to face Walt and wailed like an animal caught in a trap, *"I don't know how!"*

The rage and loneliness in the words seemed to ripple like a wave of fire in the air. It was the deep, hidden lamentation of humankind through the ages.

Tears filled Grandmother's eyes as she said, "Love be there all along. Love be in *you* but you pushed it way down so you never feel it. Love not come to you from out there," she waved her hand toward the forest, toward the world apart, "it be in you."

He held his head in his hands and blubbered, "I looked all my life...it was so hard...I never found..."

"You did find it," Grandmother answered.

He looked up at her and began to shake his head, "I never..."

"You married girl with love in her heart. Did you cherish her, return her love? You had son but you treat him just like your father treat you. You beat wife and son and they finally left you."

"No, no, it wasn't like that," he insisted hurriedly, shaking his head. "She claimed to be a good Christian woman when we married but then she turned from God. I beat them so they'd turn from their wicked ways and find Jesus."

"You be blind to who she be. You never show love. She not turn from God...she turn from you," Grandmother told him.

"There were others sent to you to help you from your darkness," Walt said. "You were offered love through your teachers, your aunt, through books placed in your hands. I sent an elderly man who offered to teach you how to garden."

"Him?" Leonard questioned sadly. "Mr. Kelly?"

"What did you say to Mr. Kelly when he said he would be glad to show you how he grew such beautiful flowers and vegetables?"

Leonard stared into space. "I remember," he said. "I was about seven, I think." He seemed to be looking into the past, seeing those word-pictures that Walt created. "I liked looking through his gate while he was working. He always sang while he worked. I liked that. I wanted to be able to do what he did...make such a beautiful garden. I thought that if I could do that where I lived then home might be nice." A whining tone had crept into his voice.

Walt nodded. "Yes, I know. What did you say to him when he came over to you at the gate and invited you in?"

Leonard's eyes looked far away, into that past, into that garden. The corners of his mouth turned down and his lips trembled. "I..."

"What, Leonard?" Walt asked.

He looked quickly up at Walt, then at Grandmother, then down again. "I...I called him a queer and I ran away." Angered by his admission, he turned his back.

Walt bent close to him, asking, "Leonard, have you no memory of Who you really are?"

Leonard turned back, frowning, suspicious. "What do you mean?"

Walt lay a hand on Leonard's shoulder but he pulled away and shivered, his face full of agony.

"You are a miracle," Walt whispered gently.

He raised his voice and cried, "You mock me!"

Walt persisted, "I want you to go back, to go within, to witness the miracle." He drew Leonard into the universe that was his body being created, into the miracle of bone and muscle and nerve, into eyes that grew vision, ears that heard sounds, a brain unspeakably deeply mysterious. He saw his birth, a new being, a new becoming. He saw his child-eyes open in wonder.

"Were you created to hate?" Walt questioned, his voice like a lullaby.

Leonard's shoulders sagged in defeat and he struggled to rise from the ground. His fire was gone as if the life force was leaking from him. He looked down at the gun, studying the weapon as if contemplating trying it on someone more vulnerable. Then he picked it up and tears ran down his cheeks as he turned and walked off down the path, moving slowly into the forest, gradually fading from sight. Not a word was spoken, our questions remained unasked. Despite the heat from the fire I shivered as I watched that lonely figure retreat from Walt and Grandmother.

Chapter 8

The Singing of the Whales

The Wheel of the Year turns and the sun's presence wanes. Darkness descends and bitter cold deepens. Ice fields overshadow golden meadows. Buds are warm thoughts in the depths of Mother Earth. Nights are lengthened and moonlight reflects on long, swordlike icicles.

Within this illusion of death Mother Earth is merely in quietude and for those who claim the Earth as their own, the moon of long nights, leafless trees in dark recesses of the forest, the drifting snowflake all tell of a spellbinding sacred beauty.

Come, dance through snowfields that have been waiting from the moment your newborn eyes opened.

Touch the One Who created the rose, the eagle, the ice crystal.

Fog swirled low over the meadow creating a cloud-like shroud around the base of the trees. It billowed through the silver grass like something arising from a place within the earth. Rain glistened and fell in droplets from the drooping evergreen branches. I could hear the foghorn sounding miles away in the Harbor. Turning my collar up I hunched my shoulders and shoved my hands deep into my jacket pockets. Only in New England, I thought. Early this morning the sun had risen with the promise of temperatures reaching fifty degrees, then by two o'clock a cold front moved in along with a raw, drizzling rain.

    I walked down my driveway and onto the road, breathing in the cold air and trying to clear my thoughts. I'd been working on a project in my studio all morning and the creative ideas were just not coming. I tried to focus and center as Walt had instructed but my mind during the past few weeks was shifting between euphoria of all the wonders I'd experienced and fear of Leonard, sort of in a manic-depressive plight. Samhain night had indeed haunted me. The sound of that gun exploding continued to reverberate in my thoughts. Leonard, so angry, so alone, walking off into the night caused me to be fearful yet sad. Hearing his wrenching confession *"I don't know how!"* when Walt asked him if he loved, gave me insight into how such a person became what he was.

    How can we judge when we haven't lived through his hell? It seemed that the more I learned the more questions, the more doubts I had. It caused me to carefully examine my own behavior and motives and the disturbing things I didn't want to see. Oh, the secrets that dwell in our memories, twisted into electrical brain-coils, reminding us chillingly of past traumas, murmuring lowly of probable horrors to come. We hold on to our tragic pasts thinking we are protecting ourselves but what we are doing is dragging imagined pain into our precious moments of possibility.

    If Leonard wasn't touched by Walt's love was there any hope for him? Nothing seemed to be resolved that night and Leonard was still out there waiting like a wounded animal. My walking meditation came to an end as I neared my house and I was eager to get inside where it was warm and cozy. I still locked up even though no one had seen nor heard of Leonard since Samhain and as I stood on the front step digging into my pocket for the key, I heard one of my cats crying on the other side of the door. I pushed Jake aside with my foot as I stepped inside. "No, you can't go out," I scolded. He dodged around me and tried to make his escape. "Come with me, you sweet old thing," I laughed as I scooped him up, groaning at his heavy weight, and leaned against the door to shut it. A bowl of milk soothed his ruffled feelings while a mug of hot coffee soothed my chills.

I went back into the studio and, after four hours, emerged to start a fire in the wood stove and light candles around the downstairs. After selecting Boston's classical station on the radio I fed the kitties then enjoyed potato pancakes and a salad as I wrote in my journal and made notes from *The Tao of Physics* by Fritjof Capra.

In showing the parallels in Eastern mysticism to modern physics he states that according to the Eastern mystics, the direct mystical experience of reality is a momentous event which shakes the very foundations of one's world view. At the end of the concluding chapter he considers the future:

I believe that the world-view implied by modern physics is inconsistent with our present society, which does not reflect the harmonious interrelatedness we observe in nature. To achieve such a state of dynamic balance, a radically different social and economic structure will be needed: a cultural revolution in the true sense of the word. The survival of our whole civilization may depend on whether we can bring about such a change. It will depend, ultimately, on our ability to adopt some of the yin attitudes of Eastern mysticism: to experience the wholeness of nature and the art of living with it in harmony.

According to ancient Chinese view, yin is the deep, intuitive, receptive female while the yang is strong, rational, aggressive male. Each contains a seed of its opposite. The balance between the two creates health and wholeness.

This search constantly amazed me. It was like a tapestry that has been woven since the Beginning in which strands from all nations and cultures intertwine in rich patterns and humanity will not see the image, the emerging whole, until it steps back to view with clear eyes. The artists, musicians, writers, poets, the philosophers, sages and seers were all part of this web. Grandmother and Walt were part of this web. The Witches of old, whose voices were almost silenced forever, spoke of this wholeness and balance. Is this the cultural revolution of which Capra writes, the Light that Walt and Grandmother tell us is now touching the world?

As I was reading and writing it occurred to me that this Light could reveal the tapestry, the universal design, and once that happened how could people continue to live "lives of quiet desperation?" I wanted to share these insights with Shelly and just as I stood to walk to the phone, it rang and was, of course, Shelly. These coincidences no longer surprised me for they seemed to occur daily, directing me to something and as parallelism would have it, she had been reading similar material from a book by Richard Bucke called, *Cosmic Consciousness*. We chatted for a while, comparing various authors, then decided to meet at the coffee shop the following Saturday, two days after Thanksgiving, to exchange books.

During the week the temperature continued to drop and snow was predicted by Saturday. When I opened my eyes Saturday morning I saw feathery flakes drifting through the air, calm and serene. I had seen this many times before—the arrival of a storm, so deceptive in its initial peaceful dance.

Before meeting Shelly I did my usual Saturday morning chores: drop books off at the library, go to recycling station, stop at the Feed & Grain Store and pick up a big bag of cat food, get gas for the car, etc., etc. Errands, I suspect are the main cause of premature aging.

They are nature's way of weeding out the weak. My lists of "things to do," if saved and placed end-to-end, would extend beyond the earth's atmosphere. The next space explorers would find scraps of paper floating about: "Pick up big bag of cat food ...Buy flea collars...Go to bank and get really big loan to buy cat stuff."

Did folks like Einstein or Gandhi do errands? Einstein's wife: "Al, quit your sitting there staring into space and take out the damned garbage!" Einstein: "Lemmie alone. I don't have time." Einstein's wife: "Don't give me that, you bum. Time is relative." Einstein: "My God! *That's it*!"

When I finally arrived at the coffee shop I grabbed my purse and the armload of books for Shelly and, hunched against the cold wind that had intensified, walked across the parking lot to the coffee shop. The familiar scents and sounds greeted me as opened the door and looked around for my friend who was waving from a booth.

"Isn't this snow wonderful?" she asked as we exchanged books.

"What's the forecast?" I asked, struggling out of my coat and settling in.

Glancing at the titles of the books, she answered, "It's not supposed to really start until later tonight. It's just going to flurry all day but tonight we're supposed to get around eight inches, more inland. I just love snowstorms, love to cozy in and have uninterrupted time at my potters' wheel. I'm in the middle of a piece that's so exciting!" She went on to explain about her creation: she had remembered my dream of Grandmother handing me the urn and from her mind's eye she had designed a two foot urn around which she would be sculpting, in half-relief, the faces of Walt, Grandmother and those shown to us when he told us he was All. It would be finished entirely in subtle earth tones and in my mind's eye I could see it and felt it would be priceless, a piece Shelly would never consider selling.

After the waitress served cups of coffee and took our order we talked about Thanksgiving Day—who we spent it with, what was served and holidays and families in general. Before the holidays my friends and I agreed that Thanksgiving would be spent with family but we would do a ceremony for Winter Solstice/Yule/Christmas. It's odd, we reflected, how the present religious days overlap the ancient days, how the Church decreed new meanings to the old ways in attempting to eradicate any belief but Christianity. The old ways only slept, waiting for a time of freedom to emerge and honor the earth and now, at the end of the millennia, before the new millennia, we can celebrate both.

Yule is a time of calling and welcoming the Light upon the earth whether it be visualized as the Sun God or the Son of God. The word Yule is ancient Anglo-Saxon meaning "wheel" referring to the Wheel of the Year, celebrated in Wiccan tradition. Christmas has been traditionally celebrated interweaving the Pagan (Pagan originally meant country dweller) with the Christian. The evergreen tree brought indoors (formerly forbidden by the Church) and decorated represents the evergreen, the non-dying of the soul, eternal Nature. The lights in windows signifies welcoming the Divine Child, the Light into our homes on this darkest night of the year's cycle.

The star in the heavens guiding the Wise Men, those ancient astrologers, on their journey, the star placed atop the Christmas tree is the same star, the pentagram, connected with Wiccan beliefs. The pentagram is a five-pointed star, each point representing the elements (earth, water, fire, air, plus spirit), often enclosed by a circle, symbolizing the Wheel of Life: birth, death, rebirth. At the center of this star is the Creator, around which all exists. Emerson, the Concord Mystic, observed this when he wrote, *"...why the star-form is so oft repeated in botany, and why the number five is such a favorite with nature..."*

I glanced out the window as the waitress refilled our cups and saw that Dorothy and Emily were walking toward the front door. Emily was leaning back, holding her tongue out to catch the snowflakes as Dorothy tried to hold her hand. Shelly turned around in the booth to see what I was smiling at, waved excitedly and immediately scooted over in the seat to make room for them.

Emily spotted us as soon as they entered, copper curls bouncing and eyes alight with joy as she hurried over waving one mittened hand. "This is the best day of all!" she exclaimed as she gave big hugs. "We're going to Plymouth to see Santa and we're going to have lunch and I got a whole ten dollars to buy Christmas gifts and I get to see *you too*!"

Dorothy smiled as she helped Emily off with her coat and said dryly, "She has a real problem showing her emotions, doesn't she?"

"Emily's like a little fairy-child going around handing out magic," I answered, snuggling up to the wiggling child as she climbed into the booth beside me and planted a noisy kiss on the end of my nose.

"Mama, can Diana and Shelly come with us today?" she asked brightly.

We began to protest, feeling that this was a special mother-daughter time but Dorothy said that it would make the day perfect. Shelly hesitated, thinking of her potters' wheel but, finally, couldn't resist Emily's pleas.

We traveled together in Dorothy's car down the expressway where, at times, russet marshland graced the landscape. After making the sharp exit to Plymouth we drove into the town's busy center then down a cobbled hill before turning onto the road that ran along Plymouth's shore. When we parked the car near the Plymouth Rock Monument and walked through the little park along the ocean we admired the replica of the Mayflower, moored by the docks for the winter, rocked on the rolling waves. I breathed the refreshing sharp tang of salt air as I noticed the white lights outlining the ship. She seemed like a beacon, calling seekers and adventurers to her as did the original Mayflower, so long ago.

We climbed the hill into the village and began to wander the cobbled streets, enjoying the sounds of Christmas carols coming from a loudspeaker at the town hall. Emily was eager to visit Santa so we found the little "gingerbread house," erected in the center of town especially for Santa each year, and waited in line for Emily to enter the magical place, to be alone with the Big Man and tell him her fondest wishes. Her turn finally came and, smiling at us and giving a little wave, she entered. Not five minutes later she emerged, holding Santa's hand. As they stepped out she said something to him that caused him to hold onto his huge pillow-belly as he leaned back and roared a genuine Santa laugh.

"I just had to meet this young lady's mother!" he exclaimed as they walked toward us.

"Oh, no." Dorothy smiled and shook her head. "What did she do?"

"Well," he began, "when she came in and sat on my lap she told me that she wanted a kitten and some books but then," he lowered his voice and said, "...then she wished something for someone named Leonard. Very strange. She said that she wished that he would find love."

Emily looked up at her mother and asked, "Was that okay to do, Mama?"

Dorothy, tears in her eyes, drew Emily close to her. "That was more than okay, Emily."

"A most remarkable child," Santa smiled. He started to leave, then turned back and said, "Oh, she gave me this." He held out his gloved hand and showed us her gift.

I gasped and reached out to lift it from his hand. I held it up to the light. I had never seen anything like it. Dorothy took it from me and looked at Emily, questioningly.

"Grandmother gave it to me," she explained, her eyes large and troubled.

"Oh, Emily, it's all right." Dorothy was quick to dispel the concern in her daughter's eyes. "I've just never seen anything like it: a quartz crystal with a tiny blue feather in it. Grandmother gave this to you? Did she say where it came from?"

Emily answered with awe, "She said it was a love-gift from Mother Earth."

Santa, hearing this, shook his head and said, "Oh, no. I cannot accept such a thing. It's a gift from her grandmother. No, please. Thank you, Emily, but that is for *you*."

"But if it's mine can't I give it to someone special?" Her eyes filled with tears.

Reaching for Santa's hand, Dorothy placed the crystal upon the white glove, closed his big hand with both of hers and said, "Emily's right. It's hers to give. Merry Christmas."

He gazed at the treasure in his hand. The crystal began to glow, pulsating with light growing stronger and stronger. His jaw dropped and he looked at us, amazed, as the glow spread to his face.

"Oh," he whispered. "Oh, this has made me so happy! This is...why am I feeling this way?" He laughed nervously and looked to Emily for the answer.

"Grandmother gave it to me and said that whoever held it would....," she paused, concentrating to remember Grandmother's exact words, "feel the joy of creation. I'm *already* happy so when I went in there," she pointed to the little Santa house, "and met you I knew you were very sad about something. That's why I gave it to you."

Shoppers passed us as we stood on the cobbled street corner, unaware of this remarkable event. Santa nodded as he caressed the crystal, still glowing, the little blue feather within seemed to be undulating as if in flight. "I *have* been sad, Emily. My wife died just a few month ago. I'm very lonely without her."

Emily nodded in understanding. "But, Santa, you'll see her again and don't you know how many people love you?" Then she leaned close to him and whispered, "I know you're not the *real* Santa. You're his helper."

He bent down and caressed her rosy cheeks and said, "I don't know how, Emily, but you seem to know a lot of things about me." He squeezed the gift in his hand and added, "I'll always treasure this. Merry Christmas, Emily." His face was rapt.

Other children were becoming impatient to visit him so we waved goodbye and he watched us as we walked away. Emily skipped ahead of us singing, unaware of the wonder that she caused. She was so genuine, so unselfconscious and life seemed to be purer wherever she was. As the rest of us stammer, stumble and struggle she simply *is*. Shelly nudged Dorothy as we walked and asked earnestly, "Does she have any idea how unique she is?"

"She's been like that since day one. If I hadn't been there I'd say she *flew* to earth," she laughed.

The afternoon was like a scene out of a Christmas movie in which everything is perfect and beautiful and human nature is showing its most loving side: a film starring Jimmy Stewart. We almost expected him to come running down the street, wishing everyone a merry Christmas. Windows of the little shops were decorated in snowy scenes, frost crystals patterning the panes of glass. Snow was beginning to gather on the evergreen garlands wound around the street lamps and upon the huge Christmas tree in the town common. Shoppers with bags and boxes laughed and sang along with the carols filling the air. When we discovered a man with a portable oven selling hot chestnuts on a street corner Dorothy said that this day had definitely been produced by Hollywood.

Hurrying from one store to another, huddled into our coats against the biting wind coming from the ocean, we made our way down the main street and onto many side streets, tiny cobbled roadways barely accommodating two cars. We would enter a shop, laughing in relief at the warm air greeting us, our cheeks red, noses sniffling and when the time came to leave we'd brace ourselves for the weather but that was part of the fun of shopping in this quaint New England town.

Toward two o'clock we stopped for lunch at "Firehouse Restaurant," an old converted fire station, and enjoyed bowls of steaming clam chowder with homemade bread. From the many-paned window by our table I watched the scene outside as I sipped my coffee, my tummy full, warm and content with this wonderful day. Emily, busy with drawing on her paper placemat, looked up and smiled as I leaned over to inspect her artwork.

"See," she said, "it's Santa with the crystal. It made him happy, didn't it?" She pointed to the crystal which was huge, almost as big as Santa. "And there's me, and you, and Shelly and Mama." We all had incredibly wide smiles as we gazed at Santa with the gigantic crystal.

"Who are those two people?" My finger went to two tiny figures at the top of the drawing, far away from the scene in the street.

"Don't you know? That's Walt and Grandmother!" She looked at me as if I had taken leave of my senses. "They were watching us."

Dorothy and I exchanged glances over Emily's head. "Did you see them?" Dorothy asked her.

Emily continued drawing, filling in colors with her box of crayons. "Sort of." She leaned back to better view her finished product. "I just know they were there."

Still curious, I questioned, "When did Grandmother give you that beautiful crystal, Emily?"

"One night."

"Why didn't you tell me about it?" her mother asked.

Emily shrugged. "It was kind of like a dream, I think. I put it in my secret hiding place and forgot about it until this morning." She put her crayons back into their box, folded her drawing then stuffed them into her little backpack. "Are we going to go soon? I still have three dollars left and have to get a present for Grammy. I saw something at that candy store that I know she'll *love*."

We left the restaurant, visited the candy shop where Emily carefully and methodically made her selection, then walked down the hill to the car. As Dorothy was unlocking the trunk to store our packages Emily turned from us, looking intently at the direction of the pier where the Mayflower was moored. "I *knew* we'd see them today!" she exclaimed and began to run toward the pier before Dorothy could stop her.

As we chased after Emily we saw them—Walt and Grandmother, sitting on the pier next to the Mayflower in the swirling snow as if it were a sunny July afternoon and they a pair of tourists. They turned their faces toward us, laughing delightedly as Emily bounded into their arms.

"This day just gets better and better!" Emily shouted as she stretched her arms to include both in her embrace.

When Shelly, Dorothy and I came near them we felt the warmth. Like a circle radiating around them the air was balmy as summer, tingling like sun's rays on our faces. They sat cross-legged on the rough wooden dock, Grandmother now holding Emily on her lap. Snowflakes were flying all around outside the circle, and it was like being enclosed in a bubble of nourishing power, watching the outside world: the opposite vision of the Christmas "snow globe."

We kissed their dear, warm cheeks and sat with them on the pier, fascinated by the enclosed radius. Dusk was closing out the daylight.

A shimmering hint of the hazy crescent moon, the moon of long nights, shone dimly behind the cloud cover. The lights in the center of town illuminated the darkening sky and the white Christmas lights outlining the Mayflower reflected off the choppy water. We could faintly hear the music playing from the speakers in the town's center, "Silent night, holy night, all is calm, all is bright…"

We sat on the pier in a circle, silent, hearing only the sounds around us. I watched Walt and Grandmother, waiting for what was to come, anticipating the wonders they would make known. A shimmering halo of light caressed Walt's body as he turned his face up to the sky. His voice was low and mysterious, resonating through me. "It is for *everyone*," he proclaimed.

I leaned closer, not sure if I had heard correctly and he continued, gazing up at the moon. "Everyone! The newborn, the old, the living, the dying. It is for the wealthy and the poor, the educated and the ones in ignorance. It is for those searching in the churches, the temples, the synagogues, the mosques as well as those searching through telescopes."

He became silent and all I could hear was the lapping of the water against the dock and the words of the carol now playing in the distance, "Oh, holy night, the stars are brightly shining…"

"What is?" I asked, my eyes blank with lack of understanding. "What is for everyone?"

He turned to me, his face radiant, glowing in the lights around us. "Why, the Light. The *Light*!" His voice rang like chimes. "Everything from the minuscule seed within the earth, to the birds and animals, to all human consciousness has been on a quest for the Light. Before the hidden atoms, before one sound, in the lonely, brittle barren starkness there was Something needing Something, love yearning to express itself."

He paused, holding his hands together as if in prayer. "With the

Word it began, for the Word was alive, throbbing with life, movement and a promise of what was to come. The Lifeseeds, male and female, quivered and filled with the power to make of Itself. Life unfolded and took on form and blossom and earth's face began to cover in lushness."

His voice continued in that hushed, awed timbre. "Through mothers' tears in numberless days, on blood-spewed battlefields, in ravenous thirst for power, in the carnage of slavery-bent people, over sad-colored flags my people have been searching. Ahhh, but now the path of savagery hesitates for an awareness, long dormant, is sparked. *The Light!* The Light awaits after eons of agony. The kingdom, the Light that you seek...it is within, it is within." His words softened to barely a whisper as he turned to each of us, his eyes like penetrating lasers.

"In this season of darkness, from the beginning of awareness, my people have called out to the Light, whether it be to the sun or the Son or to freedom, there has been that search and now," he turned his face from the moon, his eyes liquid with love, "the cycle has brought you to this point. You are ready."

Ready? Me? Oh, no! How can he say I'm ready? I'm still filled with fear and doubt. I was raised on fear, wore the wounds of fear. My parents, products of the great depression, fed me fear, it became part of my cells while in the womb. I cannot remember a carefree childhood. My parents' burden was dropped upon my shoulders before I could walk. It was a heavy, palpable heritage I carried. It was what led me on my life's spiritual search, a desperate need to find a world in which there was freedom and joy. Over the years, through trial after trial, like someone gaining strength through agonizing exercise, the fear diminished but there remained scars: fragments, mucilage holding the memory of terror. I could control it now but it was always there, waiting. Perhaps the others were ready, maybe George, certainly Emily.

Grandmother wrapped one arm around me and placed the other hand on my forehead, between my eyes. I felt a force, a flash of sparkling light inside my head, a pleasant heat. Then a peace descended upon me. It was like being new, reborn, shed of all remnants I had carried for so long. I felt light.

"What you feel be *Light*. Feel! See!" She pressed her fingers against the spot on my head while looking into my eyes.

I nodded, trying to communicate that I knew what she meant. "Yes," I sighed.

"This what Walt tell you to do...focus, focus," she firmly instructed. "This be 'third eye' where people receive Light in spiritual evolution. Brain very old, go through many changes. Human's first brain be reptilian and that be for survival. Next, mammalian brain for thinking and learning. New brain be at top of nest. This be for creating, imagining. Within brain be tiny pine cone-shaped pineal gland. This receive Light."

She released me and held my hand instead as she continued her instruction. "Though it be ancient it be long ignored because survival be most important thing to most people. Egyptians wore headdress with raised serpent's head against third eye to show wisdom emanating from this gland. East Indians paint red dot on this spot. Many ancient people paint third eye in different ways."

I remembered the blue markings on Viviane's forehead and knew that it too was evidence of ancient knowledge of this power. I was in a strange state of vast perception in which I "saw" all that Walt and Grandmother had taught us and realized that this process was both physical, emotional and spiritual. All three states were woven together like the wave and the particle of quantum physics and the picture was beginning to emerge.

Grandmother went to Shelly and Dorothy to show them as she had shown me. I lay back on the pier, staring up at the snow-filled sky, blissfully enjoying the heightened awareness, expansiveness. These emotions were not merely in my brain but in my entire self. Time was not. I throbbed with life. I listened to the music now playing in the air—Handel's "Hallelujah Chorus." Voices sang in silky, plaintive harmony. The tone wrung my heart. The music was alive and swam before my eyes. It whispered and swirled, pierced the darkness with Light. Rhythms rippled and complex patterns danced into being. Flute-tones sighed sweet-measured promises as the voices ascended in joy, "Hallelujah, Hallelujah!"

Had I ever really *heard* music before this? The sounds entered me, were a part of me. Grandmother clasped my hand and slowly drew me from the music.

"Learning to live in both worlds be very difficult," she said. "Through all centuries there be ones who knew. They learn balance and they go out into world but then have to go off by themselves to forest or mountain top. World can take great toll on ones who see. Time in solitude, in nature restore them and give them strength to go back. If they not spend time alone they in great danger."

Do I want this? Yes, this bliss is where I want to be but how to leave this and go back to ordinary life. How can one perform the mundane tasks that life requires? How can one work in a mindless job, be in the world of commerce with its heartlessness and greed? How to associate with people who have no awareness of *this Light*? As I came back to the world, allowed my mind to chase a negative stream of consciousness, the peace vanished. I felt heavy, encased in flesh.

"Grandmother tell you before—you on hardest path. Even in Light you still hold onto fear, hmmm? She patted my hand in assurance, "That be okay. You see. It all be part of process, of evolution and, remember, you not alone. This be happening to people all over the world."

Walt began to answer some of our questions. "As Grandmother has said, it is a process. You will learn, and we will help you to navigate life in this new awareness. Yes, the path is most difficult but it is the process that gives you the needed strength and wisdom. You are viewing what is to come as a child views ordinary life. She wonders how she will ever do all the things she sees adults doing. She fears she is not smart enough to go through college and receive a degree, secure a job that will pay enough to afford food and housing and all life's necessities. The child's fears come from her ignorance of her growing strengths. She sees not the process but only the desired outcome and, of course, feels inadequate from her child's viewpoint.

"So too, you see your path and it causes you apprehension but each step on the path takes you one step out of ignorance. The wisdom you will gain will allow you to function in the world, will show you ways to meet life's necessities without working in a job you abhor and will fill your hearts with love and compassion for every living thing."

As I lay on the pier listening to Walt and gazing at the sky above I thought of Van Gogh's mystical painting "Starry Night" and of his tormented life. Why, I wondered, is it so difficult for those creative souls, for the ones who see so deeply and so true? Why were the ones who had the most to give the ones who were persecuted or ignored? So often they lived in misery and poverty as they struggled to live and listen to beauty's call. It is as true today as it was in the day of Van Gogh or Michelangelo or Mozart.

Walt touched my face and I turned to him. Within his eyes seemed to lie the answers. He smiled and asked, "What is your life's work?"

I struggled to focus my mind on his words. "Life's work?" I repeated.

He nodded. "Where is your heart? Where do you wander in your dreams? Where do you loose yourself and merge with that which is greater?"

I didn't have to ponder the answer. I answered immediately, "Art, writing."

"Ahhh, yes. Then that is your call."

"But, Walt, it's not that easy. Oh, *you know*. When I was raising my children there was very little money and life was so hard. Worrying about paying bills and buying food is *not* very spiritual and I don't want to go through that again. Being able to earn enough money in any of the arts is almost impossible. I…"

He put one finger to my lips to hush my resistance. I lay my face against his chest and felt embarrassed. Will these fears never leave me? The glow that filled me with Grandmother's touch had vanished as the apprehension entered. Shelly and Dorothy shared my anxieties, I knew. We sat in a circle, within our warm bubble and only Emily seemed to be free of the concerns most adults experienced.

Grandmother took my hand and drew me close, pulling me into her strength. Her soul was in the ancient world, a time when humans were the caretakers and talked with the animals and could hear the song of the universe. That was the time of our innocence when wolves ran in wild places and owls cruised on currents. I wondered if this spoke of the Biblical story of our fall from paradise. Perhaps, once upon a time, we knew as children seem to know and forget only as we grow to adulthood. We evolved through hungry needs. Life seemed, at once, precarious, fragile and wondrous.

"Mmmmm," she mused. Her warmth was comforting. "It be true that some ancients knew but for most it be just survival. Evolution never easy, always big struggle but evolution now be beyond struggle to eat. It be struggle to find self, find Creator. It be struggle to heal planet. When Light touch life it make big change it heart. Grandmother can't tell you what your life's work be. That be for you to know but I can make promise that you soon find way and I give warning that it not be easy to walk on new path, to break out of old system."

"Why? You keep saying that! Why does it have to be hard to go to something better?"

"When you try to leave path everyone else on they try to pull you back. Some just feel scared for you and say, 'You can't do that! It can't be done! This be way things be. You crazy!' They tell you things like that. Then maybe you listen and get scared and worry. 'Maybe they right,' you think. 'Maybe I better stay where I am. I better stay safe.' Many people have dreams, start to travel new path but when things get shaky they run back to old prison so they be safe."

I thought about what she said. It was true. When I left the world of advertising agencies to start my own business everyone said those very words: "It can't be done." But this is even more shaky. I was considering dropping out entirely, with *nothing* to go to.

She chuckled softly and said, "It be like jumping out of plane. You have faith that parachute open. This be same thing. You have faith that arms of Great Spirit be there to catch you, to guide you. It be scary at first but then you find you always safe and pretty soon you jumping all the time and it be fun!"

Well, I thought, I'm not sure "it be fun." I'd settle for it be safe.

"You be under spell," Grandmother smiled, shaking a finger at me. "I tell you before that you be like king who thinks he be pauper and wanders around seeking when all the while he have everything. He be under spell and not know Who he be. You be like that. For so long, for many, many centuries people be taught that life be so hard, be filled with pain and hunger and all kind of horrible things like that but everything be here for them! All food, all shelter, all beauty, all love. It all be waiting to be accepted. It be fear that keep *everyone* so blind. Yes, it be fear that drive ones who are mean and greedy and take from others. It be fear that cause hardhearted business people to trample over others. It be fear that cause some governments to enslave people.

"You see what fear do to *you* who have kind hearts? Just imagine what it do to someone who have no love in heart. You feel peace when Grandmother touch you, show you place in brain to open and you feel that peace leave when fear come in. This be where you get stuck and what you must change now. It be big hurdle to jump over, hmmmm?"

As she talked her tiny hand occasionally patted mine, a nurturing gesture that I found comforting. "Spiritual evolution happening. Practice letting fear go and flow into new path. Look at big view here. Look at history. Look at own history in America. Those wise people who wrote your Declaration of Independence and Constitution—they saw far into future. They had vision of new path called 'democracy.' They even put mystical symbols on money. Look at dollar bill and you see pyramid with third eye over it. They knew that America be big step in evolution. When people came over in Mayflower," she gestured at the replica in the ocean beside us, "they be seeking religious freedom. Oh, but then they make big mistake and, because of fear, try to force their 'freedom' onto everyone else."

She chuckled at humanity's foolishness, then continued. "But founding fathers be very wise and know people's foolishness when they form democracy. In looking back can you see evolution? Can you see that over many years, oh, such great changes happen? Days of children toiling in factories be over, days of women being property of husband be over, days of people brought here from Africa in chains of slavery be over. You see? Democracy finally be starting to work. Oh, it not solve every little thing right now. People have to grow up to fit into this big idea."

I thought about what she said but also remembered the racism, sexism and child abuse which still existed. I thought of the abuse of power in governments, the staggering crime rate, the poverty, which drove people to hatred. She nodded in understanding and said, "Don't look only at what still be wrong. See, instead, what be right, what be changed. This be evolution. Evolution take long time. It be same for all religions too. Jesus gave people wonderful message *two thousand years ago* and people just beginning to understand. He came as Light at that time. He come to enlighten people but they not be ready then. We come now and people be little bit wiser and it not take so long this time."

"Grandmother," Shelly protested, "even if it takes *half* that time, a thousand years, we'll either blow ourselves up or we'll poison ourselves from the face of the planet. Even fifty years will be too long!"

Grandmother touched Shelly to reassure her. "All things on earth be peoples' choice. This be free will. In last thirty years many, many be calling out, searching. These be ready and be touched by Light. This why it not take fifty years even. Grandmother tell you this before. It be happening now, today, *tonight*. Things going to start balancing and when that happen even those with hard hearts be touched."

"Will this lead to paradise here on earth?" Dorothy asked hesitantly.

"Paradise? What be paradise? What you live in now be paradise to people that first winter after they land in what now be America. When people got off Mayflower and almost starved. Many died. That first winter life be terrible. Oh, if they could have seen what you have now they think it be big paradise. You have much good food, nice home, warm clothes. You be healthy. Hmmmm? Oh, they would have thought you live in some kind of heaven. You see?

"Humans strive upward. As they strive they solve problems but, as I tell you before, this always have shadowside. It be this way all through history. Human mind capable of so much, create so much but every new thing brings new problems. How you think world be learning? You do this, you do that and pretty soon you get scared and say, 'Oops, doing that made big problem!' She threw up her hands with exaggerated shock, pantomiming our dismay. "Then you have to find better way."

I smiled despite my feelings of frustration. This seemed to go in circles: problems, solutions, problems, solutions. "It all sounds like the Sorcerer's Apprentice," I commented.

"What that be?" Grandmother looked at me with curiosity.

I explained the story of Mickey Mouse's dilemma of using magic to get the brooms in motion and then not having the knowledge of how to stop them.

"That be it. You be like that Mouse fellow not knowing how to fix troubles and things get all in big scary mess."

"So, what difference does it make if the Light touches people and things begin to balance? This will just lead to more problems, won't it?"

"That be true." Her eyes shone and she smiled wisely.

I shrugged my shoulders and gestured helplessness. "Then why…"

"Oh, you be so blind sometimes!" She fluffed her shawl around her shoulders and frowned. Emily giggled at Grandmother's ferocious expression. In her childlike innocence she had total faith in these two old ones and a trust that they could never truly be angry. Grandmother's face softened as she looked down at Emily. "You think Grandmother be funny, hmmm?" Emily only smiled as she toyed with the fringe on Grandmother's shawl.

"Now, where Grandmother be before she get laughed at?" she muttered, attempting once again to appear stern. "This be *life,*" she continued. "Life be evolution. Life be growing. Shadowside push you to grow. Think of life and evolution as ladder and this ladder start with first humans and go upward to the Divine. Ladder have maybe billions of rungs to climb. Humans right now on about tenth rung of ladder. You always think you soooo far up ladder. You just beginning. You see how it be?"

I imagined the infinite ladder and we fragile humans teetering on the first rungs, always assuming we have reached the ultimate. What lie ahead? What unimagined experiences and discoveries waited? Perhaps the mysteries that quantum physics was peeking into were only a doorway cracking open and what lie beyond that opening was the ineffable, too voluminous for words.

My mind wandered, felt drawn out of my body and an unaccustomed awareness showed me a future in which we would look back on this present time as dark and barbaric. It was a luminosity born out of an immense, massive darkness. I experienced this future as one reborn, like a hatchling, air sensitive, touch sensitive, sound sensitive fanning my filament wings. In this floating awareness I heard the voices of Grandmother and Walt. They were instructing us, thousands upon thousands of humans, to feel, to see, to know Who we are—we are primordial divinity. I knew we were to accomplish this great leap in our lives. We were to embrace the Light in solitude and meditation. Walt's voice rang in my ear, "Listen! Be silent and listen to the Wisewoman within. She will be with you, will guide your feet and hands." I heard Grandmother's silvery laughter.

When I opened my eyes our teachers were gone and the snow swirled around us, sparkling like sugar under the lights of the Mayflower. I smiled at my friends and knew they had journeyed with me. Once more we heard the voices of music pouring over the town and something else, something deeper.

    We heard the sounds of whales singing through the dark depths of the ocean around us, into the air around our planet.

Chapter 9

The Paradigm Shift

Our quiet footsteps, muffled by deep winter, take us to the darkest hour. On that bitter, icebound night the sun's return is solemnized and celebrated. The longer days may continue in glacial bleakness but beating hearts know the season's tide has turned.

So, too, is humankind's tide turning. The hour seems so dark but in this instant the shadow-dreams of life are suspended and our tenuous floating planet hangs mute and trembling. Light hovers across earth's shivering skin. It awaits. It warms. It loves.

My dreams were filled with magnificent images, barely remembered upon waking. They left me with a hopeful joy. As I opened my eyes the morning after my day in Plymouth I turned to the window by my bed and watched the diminishing snowfall, occasional fluffy flakes drifting through the air and landing on the white blanket that had fallen through the night. I pondered on our wonderful night and the harmony of the whales' chanting in the sea, an ancient enchantment from a dark and shrouded mystery that holds tales of our past. As we drove home through the storm, the snow in the headlight's beam gave the illusion of rushing through the stars in space.

Indeed, we had felt like space explorers, witnessing outside known reality. On this morning I felt like a child on Christmas Eve, on the edge of the miraculous. Oh, this day, this gift! My cats were curled up around me, their little bodies vibrating with purring and kneading the blankets, eyes half-closed in ecstasy, wearing little Buddha-smiles. Did they feel what I was feeling and was this their natural state or were they bathing in the glow that was inside me? When I sat up and swung my legs over the side of the bed they stood and stretched luxuriously. Then all three stood outside the shower, occasionally attempting to shove the glass door open so they could peek in to watch the odd display inside, impatiently waiting for me to finish my absurd human activities so they could have breakfast.

The scene from my kitchen window was breathtaking. About eight inches of powdery snow lay across the meadow beyond and every tree and bush was alight as the sun began to filter through the clouds. Hundreds of birds fluttered around the bird feeders, rising and falling in their ornithological ballet. I could hear them chattering, fluttering, twittering. Three pairs of red cardinals and many blue jays added their vibrant plumage to the dance and a covey of quail made their way, in formation, from the meadow to the area below the feeders where seed lay scattered. It was a scene that, if painted, would be too perfect, too flawless.

The power of my feelings was causing me to feel giddy. So much to see, so much to feel, so much to do. The Light that Grandmother had shown me when she touched between my eyebrows, the "third eye," was softly pulsating, warm with love, an afterglow throbbing in my blood. I wanted to embrace the world. I wanted to wander the streets, hug people and shout, like a demented prophet, "You...oh, look at you! See how wonderful you are!" I smiled but shuddered at the thought of becoming like Leonard, a raving fanatic.

The aroma of coffee as it brewed was startling. Had it always smelled this wonderful? I marveled. It's taste was ambrosia as I held the warm cup and watched the birds feeding. The birds were feathered light, defying gravity. My senses were so heightened that every experience felt almost orgasmic. I *knew*, beyond any doubt, that the Light, this Light was within *me*. Grandmother hadn't put it there but she had made me aware of it. Her cosmic nudge had awakened it, fanned the spark into this radiance.

As I dressed to go outdoors, pulling on my boots, jacket, hat and mittens, time seemed to have altered. Even in my excitement I felt leisurely, like I had all the time in the world, that time was not and experience was all. When I opened the back door, for the first time in months I had no inclination to lock it. I knew I was safe. The cold air hit me in a blast of exhilaration as I inhaled and filled my lungs. The act of breathing, of gulping in the atmosphere, this unconscious thing we did thousands of times every day, was now a gift and I laughed aloud. Such wonder!

Holding my arms up to the sky I pirouetted until I fell into the bed of snow. I lay there, waiting for the spinning to subside, and began to examine the frozen crystals on my mitten. Turning my hand and contemplating the delicate designs, I wondered how this was possible. My mind probed for the answer, for the reasoning, for the Creator behind these lacy masterpieces but mind alone cannot fathom. Mind must surrender and allow, not answers and reasons, but the joy of the mystery to sink into the bones.

I sat up and birds began to alight around me, hopping closer and closer until I was surrounded. Slowly, I held my hand out and a crow came to rest there. He cocked his head and seemed to stare into my eyes. I felt a strange bond with him, as if he knew me and I him—Brother Crow. Making his way up my arm he came to perch on my shoulder and leaned close to my face as if he had a secret to tell. With a loud cry he pulled out a strand of my hair and flew off, flapping his wings and calling out his triumph like laughter. I was so startled I lay back in the snow and joined his raucous laughter, rubbing my temple where he had plucked his treasure.

I remembered something from one of the Wicca books Shelly had shown me. "The Calling of the Animals" was a ritual of the ancients who knew their oneness with all creatures. The Native Americans also had this ritual for their hunt. They honored the animal before it was killed for survival and they claimed that the animal knew of his part in the hunt and gave himself. The hunter would humbly thank the slain animal's spirit and would eat its flesh in reverence. I'm not sure that any animal willingly sacrifices itself for humans but at least the old civilizations *considered* the emotions of their animal brothers and sisters. Today we have little empathy for anything that doesn't look like us. Even our fellow humans are not exempt from our belief that varied shades of skin place people higher or lower on our warped scale of what is goodness, what is intelligent.

Were these birds honoring what was now in me, this throbbing Light? I stood and they fluttered around me, settling on my shoulders as I walked to the meadow. At the edge of the meadow I stopped and looked into the forest which appeared to be under a magic spell now with its silver-laden trees. I thought of the ritual of the calling of the animals and sent waves of love and Light into the place before me. Sunlight fell in rays through the trees and onto the ground where it lay across the lustrous snow in sharp lines as though it came from under the snow, from the earth's interior, trying to shine out. I chanted to the animals, experiencing waves of strange emotions. The vibration in my throat seemed to bubble up from an ancient memory, drawn from my genetic spiral ladder.

And they came. Tentatively, at first, they began to emerge from dark and hidden places, places forbidden to all except those who descried their language. Squirrels scurried down trees, chattering, their tails flipping in excited communication. A pair of raccoon lumbered toward me, their comical masked faces looking up at me questioningly. A red fox appeared, shoving her delicate snout into a mound of snow then quickly lifting her head, sending the flakes flying as she snapped at the air. Our eyes met and she wriggled like a puppy, inviting me to play before she leaped into the air, turned, and trotted into the forest, her plumed tail waving a farewell.

The trees whose roots sank deep into the frozen earth seemed to respond to my touch and my sleeping herbs in the blanketed gardens knew their time of rebirth would be signaled by the sun's message. It seemed almost as if I could call the rose up through the snow crystals and watch its fragrant blossoming. As geese flew over the treetops in chevron formation, searching for a landing site, a doe, heavy with her unborn fawn, stepped delicately from behind thick foliage, pawed at the ground and raised her head to me. Her eyes were dark and deep and full of forest lore. She stepped closer and I remained very still, sending her warm thoughts. Nuzzling my jacket, she butted her head against me and allowed my hand to touch her flank. I stood in this timeless moment until the creatures, my brothers, my sisters, wandered away. These were the experiences of the mystics. A musician, perhaps Delius, could have spread this experience onto a sheet of paper, into the symbols of black notes but I, I could only feel humbly honored.

When do we become trapped, I wondered? When do people stop living in joy? Do we realize what we are doing when we turn from the wonder and begin the long trudge into what we are taught is responsible adulthood? We never realized back then what we were releasing when we last ran barefoot through tall, wet grass or when we leisurely walked, unconscious of others' opinions, through an afternoon rain. Most of us live as strangers to ourselves, to the mysteries at dawn, to the interior of flowers. Can we recognize that prodigious time of entrapment so that we can guard against succumbing?

Can we take the children with us on journeys of wonder? Can we teach them to never give in to the mass consciousness of the mundane?

Slowly, I began to walk back to my house and as I walked through the meadow where tufts of golden grass were bent under the weight of snow, I heard voices and, as my house came into view, saw my friends.

"We were just about to follow your footsteps in the snow to find you!" Jeff said, ruffling my hair.

"You wouldn't believe what's been happening to me," I confided breathlessly as I leaned against him. I knew from the looks on everyone's faces that it was time to brew a big pot of coffee and sit by the fire for a chat. Don and Jeff carried logs up from the basement, got a fire going and we began speaking of the wondrous things we all were feeling and the experiences each of us had been having. Dorothy had tried to call me on the phone and when she couldn't reach me she called Shelly and they met at the coffee shop and, as our lives seemed to be lived in coincidences these days, Don, Jeff, Robert and George walked in. The men, on that previous night, had also been with Grandmother and Walt. This, we deduced, was evidence of the theory of "non-locality" in quantum physics theory; things are instantaneously everywhere. They had gone to The Cliffs together, had met our teachers, been filled with the Light and had heard the whales singing that resonant deep poetry and this morning we were all living in the mystical afterglow, sparkling with childlike liberation.

"There must be pockets of people all over the world this morning dizzy with happiness," Robert concluded, giving me a hug as we stood together in front of the wood stove, warming our backsides. Through the afternoon we shared our stories, enjoyed lunch, drank rich, dark coffee, played in the snow and basked in the perfect sun-dappled afternoon.

The days that followed were spent mostly in solitude and meditation. The dizzy euphoria ebbed and settled into contentment. I continued to work in my studio, consult with clients and the dissatisfaction I'd been experiencing waned and was replaced with observance. It was like I was two people, one working and the other watching. The part of me that looked on saw the source of dissatisfaction but knew I would be guided to a new path, one that would bring deep contentment.

Preparations for the holidays began to fill my days. It had always amazed me that there were so many people who disliked this season because it was too commercial. Somehow, I had always managed to bypass the commercialism that was, indeed, rampant and create joyful rituals. The secret, I believed, was to slow down and do only what creates joy, every act leading up to the Celebration of the Light done with mindfulness. There ought to be a manual for us to follow entitled, *The Tao of Christmas*.

My business always slowed down right before the holidays and instead of worrying as was my usual tendency, I enjoyed the open time. I shopped in little villages, selected my tree and decorated it (with help from my cats), placed white lights in my windows, hung my wreath on the front door, wrapped presents (with help from my cats), watched all the traditional shows on TV and listened to the Christmas music that everyone listened to year after year. My friends and I spent many hours enjoying long walks in the woods and by the ocean, despite the biting cold. Emily constantly amazed us and taught us the importance of retaining that childlike wonder and wisdom. She was our little Buddha and when we'd get upset over something she'd say, "That's the Way it is." It was always Emily who reminded us to remember what Walt and Grandmother had taught us and encouraged us to medicate and listen for the Voice. We listened, we heard and knew "the Way it is."

Christmas Eve was clear and bitter cold and we entered the warmth of the church with relief. The interior of the old Unitarian church was elegant in its beautiful simplicity and I sat quietly with my friends watching other people entering. The voices coming from the choir loft, like invisible angels, sang of the mystery of this celebration and the glow of candles softened every face that looked toward the pulpit. The minister, an eloquent speaker and gifted storyteller, mesmerized us with his words. New England was at her winter best on the drive home as stars twinkled in the cold-bright sky and the homes we passed seemed settled in for the night, protecting the occupants from the cold and dark. White lights shined from windows and bright-colored lights covered bushes and fences.

When we arrived back home and walked through the door, the lingering smells of baking reminded me that a big apple pie had been set aside for an after-church snack. Soon the scent of brewing coffee brought everyone into the kitchen where we consumed the entire pie and talked about the sermon we'd heard earlier. The minister had spoken of the Light and of its importance in the coming year. His eyes seemed to meet ours as he spoke and I wondered if he was one visited by Grandmother and Walt.

Emily stood, mesmerized by my tree, admiring the birds I had placed on the branches amid the tiny white lights. There were cardinals, doves, blue jays, bluebirds, quail, chickadees, tiny owls and on the top of the tree was a crow with a red ribbon and a spring of holly around his neck. I had been delighted when I found him in a gift shop and, even though he cost more than I wanted to spend, I bought him in honor of Brother Crow who'd made off with a strand of my hair. What did he do with it, I wondered? Is it tucked into his nest somewhere at the top of a tall spruce tree? The thought pleased me.

After exchanging gifts we sat by the fire, our bellies full, feeling sleepy and contented. Emily sat on her mother's lap leafing through a book George had given her and Jeff, Don and Robert sang carols as George plunked haltingly on the out-of-tune piano, laughing as they forgot most of the words, substituting many "la la las."

When the men tired of their performance they joined us by the fire. As I got up to put a CD on to play I passed the living room window and a sound caught my attention. Icicles falling? I glanced out the window but saw nothing and as I was about to walk away the sound returned. I bent close to the pane where the electric candle gave some illumination and cupped my hands around my eyes for better vision. A movement caught my eye and as I looked down into the flower box outside the window, now filled with snow, I saw him. Brother Crow was perched in the flower box.

"What are you doing?" Dorothy asked.

I burst out laughing and called for them to come over. Everyone gathered by the window and Brother Crow seemed agitated at our poor manners as we stared at him. "Maybe he's the crow I was telling you about," I said, still peering through the window. "Do you think he wants to come in and join his friend at the top of the tree?"

George opened the door and stepped out, leaning toward the flower box. My ebony friend, waiting for this invitation, fluttered to him and dropped the gift at his feet. "What is it?" I asked from the open door as he stooped to retrieve it.

"Oh, my God!" I gasped, as George somberly held out the object and silently met my eyes. It was Leonard's cross.

"What is it?" everyone asked, as he came back inside and shut the door. He calmly showed them the cross and, like the silver cross displayed to ward off evil, they stepped back and held their breath. He walked to the coffee table and set the cross upon it, absentmindedly wiping his hands on his pants. Emily reached for it and her mother stepped forward with a warning, "Emily, don't!"

"It's only Leonard's cross," she objected.

"Still…" Dorothy insisted, holding her daughter's shoulder firmly, "don't touch it."

I walked back to the window and looked out, almost expecting to see Leonard's gaunt face staring at me. No one was there and Brother Crow had flown away.

"This is ridiculous," I muttered. "He probably lost it the night he was here, Samhain night. He had to have walked through the yard to get back to the road. Crows are notorious for finding shiny objects."

"Don't you think it's a pretty weird coincidence that a crow should find it, tap on your window on Christmas Eve then drop it next to George?" Jeff questioned. "I mean, man, look at all that's happened to us. *Nothing's* a coincidence anymore!"

"Are we to believe that a crow is giving us some kind of message?" Don asked skeptically, picking up the cross, turning it over to examine both sides.

"Are we to believe that two old people come to us and teach us, are we to believe that we heard the whales singing, that the animals came out of the woods when Diana called?" Jeff threw back, his anger rising.

"Remember…" Emily cautioned us.

We turned to her and waited. Her eyes were big and sad. "Remember what, Emily?" I asked, impatience sounding in my voice.

"You keep forgetting!" she answered, almost in tears. "Remember what they told us about being afraid." Her lip quivered and she whispered, "Remember the *Light*."

We glanced at each other guiltily then began to relax. "She's right," George said, as his own eyes filled with tears. He sat in his favorite chair by the fire. "Let's just calm down and think about this."

Emily nodded and joined him in the chair, leaned against his chest and held his gnarled old hand. He smiled at her then continued, staring fixedly at the flames. "Jeff's right too, you know. Coincidences aren't just coincidences anymore. We're in another place now. I'm surprised we fall back so easily." He hesitated, embarrassed, and took a deep breath.

I didn't want that object in my home. It was *his,* had been worn next to his body and, in my mind, I felt that his foulness must have entered the very atoms of it. Emily had said that it was just Leonard's cross. No, it was part of him.

Without thinking further I picked it up and as I walked to the wood stove and opened the door to the flames George said, "Don't."

I turned and questioned him with my eyes. "Oh, Diana, don't you see?" he asked. "You're giving him power. You're giving *it* power." He pointed to the cross I was holding warily between two fingers, as if trying to avoid contamination. "I admit that when I saw the cross I thought that man was back but it's only something he wore. Nothing more. It can't hurt us. If a message is being sent to us we'll find out what it is when it's time. Until then let's do what Emily reminded us to do. Let's remember the Light. It's Christmas Eve," he gestured toward the tree in the corner. "Let's continue our celebration. *This* is what it's all about! It's knowin' that when we think the dark's here all we have to do is turn to the Light."

I opened my hand and looked down at the offending object. A cross made of wood and metal. An object that had caused controversy for two thousand years. An object that caused feelings of horror when it was used as an instrument of torture. An object that some loved, others feared and a few made a symbol of hate and intolerance. I opened the front door and laid it back into the flower box by the window. Maybe Brother Crow would take the hint and hide it deep in the woods somewhere.

No one said a word and I sat in one of the big wingback chairs by the fire. George closed his eyes in meditation. Emily was lying against him, her eyes half-shut as she drifted into sleep. The room became quiet. I shut my eyes and heard the comforting sound of the fire crackling, the purr of the air blowers on the wood stove, the Christmas music playing and small household noises. Warmth began to fill the spot between my eyebrows and a blanket of peace slowly descended upon me. I released a heavy sigh and fell deeper and deeper into a timeless zone, drawing and absorbing energy. Words began to form, whispers echoed, whispers of the voices of the ancients, the trumpeting of elephants, the singing of the whales. They joined in a euphonious chorus of encouragement.

A vision began to fill my spiritual sight and I saw all the stars in the heavens gather into one. Within this one glorious light there were beings who looked out from the luminescence. These beings at one time walked upon the earth and I recognized each for who they were when they existed here. Oh, within this light there were so many, thousands upon thousands who had lived on this good earth and raised us higher for their lives: ancient sages and prophets, musicians, writers, artists, poets, scholars, scientists, healers, holy men and women, children.

The essence of every living species dwelt within this star, their pattern and code forever conscious: the desert's coyote spirit, the tundra's polar bear, the island's sea lion, the parrot and primate spirits of the rain forest, the snow leopard and grizzly bear of the mountains, the savanna's zebra, lion and elephant, the buffalo spirits from the grassland and the whale and dolphin spirits of the oceans. All life was contained in this star, our origin, our destiny.

I heard George's voice murmur, "Oh, oh, the star...ohhhh." He sighed and his breath swirled within the resonance of the chanting. The entire universe, from the smallest insect to the unseen galaxies, was interdependent, woven together in one intricate pattern.

We reached across the timeless for That which loves us.

Chapter 10

The Healing

There is a chill wind rising in a shadowed place.
It prowls in the quiet predawn hush.
The night has been heavy in its expectation
Waiting for this time of transmutation
Where the fundamental point of matter,
The center of the atom
Mid clouds of electrons,
Listens for the sound spilled through the Light.

Deep winter was upon us and the world was quiet in my acre as I stepped outside into the glacial air and walked carefully down the steps and the slippery driveway to my car. Layers of ice and snow crunched under the tread of my boots and I cringed as the cold drew the warmth from my body, a cold that chilled the marrow. When I opened the car's door it creaked loudly as if in protest to being awakened. I started the motor and turned the heat on as I scraped the windows. While hacking the encrusted glass I thought of summer, of greeting the dawn by walking barefoot through the wet grass. I thought of the scent of warm earth, of gardens bent under dew, of roses and butterflies and the glittering, thundering ocean. It's coming, I thought as ice slid down my sleeve. A few more months, I groaned as a sudden wind sprayed snow crystals over my face and down my neck. I stamped my feet and clapped my mittened hands to shake the ice and snow from me and slid into the driver's seat. The heat was just beginning to warm the car as I turned the radio to the classical station, broke my way through the driveway and began my treacherous drive over roads not yet plowed or sanded.

As I drove, the dove-gray morning light was ignited as cloud-cover blew to the east and the sun shone through. The winter world became magical as iced telephone wires, trees, bushes and every object under the sun suddenly blazed into brilliant flame and I nearly drove off the road in my stupefaction. Winter definitely had its compensations, I thought: cozy fires, being safe yet snowbound as a raging storm piled snow two feet high and these occasional brilliant crystalline ice-shows.

Christmas was over and tonight people would be celebrating New Year's Eve and then it would be back to harsh reality for most. This year I wouldn't experience the usual melancholy. I had Walt and Grandmother. I had the singing of the whales, the calling of the animals. I knew that the magic never had to end. I knew about the Holy Women, the ancient ones. I knew about unordinary powers. This year I knew joy.

Christmas Eve's vision-star seemed to be etched upon my forehead like the blue tattoo on the Wise Woman Viviane. Its radiance instructed me, softened my heart so that I began to empathize with every creature. Television's news programs displaying humanity's monstrous face also revealed a species that had it within them to be noble. Walt and Grandmother had shown me the way to see that monstrous face yet to look deeply, beyond the appearance, beyond the pictures of pain and the ghastly deeds and to witness the seeds of life. This empathy, they had said, was not to excuse those who caused pain but instead would lead to understanding the importance of this—that every infant born must be welcomed in wonder and delight. It is not an argument between ProChoice and ProLife. This will not happen through judicial decree or guilt but only when the parents are spiritually prepared. Every child that comes here from the ocean of the infinite has the right to claim this planet as her home, as her rich heritage. A child not welcomed suffers in a loveless world. A child that is welcomed will be whispered to at the stunning instant of her advent, when her first cry spills through the dawn, "You come to us as a miracle, you come to us as spirit into flesh."

Wordsworth's poem speaks of our origin:

> *Our birth is but a sleep and a forgetting:*
> *The soul that rises with us, our life's star,*
> *Hath had elsewhere its setting,*
> *And cometh from afar:*
> *Not in entire forgetfulness,*
> *And not in utter nakedness,*
> *But trailing clouds of glory do we come*
> *From God, who is our home:*
> *Heaven lies about us in our infancy!*
> *Shades of the prison-house begin to close*
> *Upon the growing boy.*

As I drove through the Harbor that one line kept repeating itself in my mind: *trailing clouds of glory do we come.* Few cars were traveling the Harbor's icy roads as the sun rose over the sleepy ocean village on a holiday morning and I was able to park directly in front of The Mooring Diner. I left the car's motor running while I carefully made my way to the front door. Sparkling icicles above the entrance threatened to cascade upon me as I tugged on the door and stepped inside. I was immediately surrounded by warmth, aromas of breakfasts cooking and remnant sounds of Christmas carols.

Where are the clouds of glory, I thought, as I watched an elderly man, toothless and emaciated, surreptitiously pour alcohol from a tiny bottle into his coffee? He glanced around, hunched guardedly over his drink, and licked his lips in anticipation. After nearly draining the cup, he wiped his mouth with the back of his hand and our eyes met. Where are your clouds of glory, my eyes asked? He frowned and turned his head away, holding onto his cup and staring vacantly out the window at the churning ocean. What does he see? Can he see the ocean that I see, the ocean turning gold with the morning sun? If he does how can he continue living in his dark world?

The waitress interrupted my thoughts by sliding the container of coffee across the countertop and asking for the money. When I pulled the heavy door open and stepped outside I saw the haggard face of the man looking sadly through the window at me. His eyes seemed to say, "If you can't give me your ocean, don't judge me. Clouds of glory? Remember...*shades of the prison house.*" The voice of winter roared through the Harbor and, by the pier's edge, set the masts' rigging to play a plaintive song.

I drove to the Lighthouse which kept sentinel at the end of Shore Drive and pointed the car toward the golden ocean where seagulls, wings aflame, soared low over the icy dazzle of the receding tide. A man, encased in layers of wool, scurried on his hands and knees over the glazed rocks with camera in hand focusing on the frozen scene before him. On the car radio a women was speaking of the approaching new year, of resolutions, of hope. I sipped my coffee and thought, "Oh, if she could know what's bubbling in the cosmos."

Later, following Shore Drive back into the Harbor, I stopped at the video store to rent a film, went to the library and searched the shelves until I selected a pile of promising books then stopped at the bakery for some treats to enjoy during my New Year's Eve solitary celebration. As the morning advanced the sun climbed the sky then hid behind the forming dark clouds. The temperature began to plummet and by noon it was dark and ominous, the morning's fairyland vanished. Back home I settled in, looking forward to the pleasure of a long cozy afternoon and evening.

I sank into the couch, curling up under an afghan, three cats surrounding me, fitting themselves expertly amid the lumpy terrain. Library books were piled up on the floor beside me, a cup of mocha on the coffee table, radio playing softly, wood stove fire cheerfully warming the room. Through the window I gazed transfixed at the naked trees rattling and creaking against the winter twilight sky. Frost-fronds were beginning to pattern the window panes. The frozen scene, the darkened corners hid the fact that something wonderful was happening beneath the surface. Deep in the bones of Mother Earth inexplicable things were filled with astounding, intensely conscious life in that dark, forbidden realm where the land has her secret places. The keening wind sang her aria as night descended and January's Wolf Moon took shape in the sky. I closed the book that I had held opened in my hands and remembered lines from *The Day is Done* by Longfellow:

> *The day is done, and the darkness*
> *Falls from the wings of Night,*
> *As a feather is wafted downward*
> *From an eagle in his flight.*

My eyes closed and the book dropped to the floor beside me. The wind's song carried me to dreams. The wind's song was a voice speaking of strength, of honor. It chanted and that intonation painted a vision in my mind, black and swirling. The black robes of Viviane swirled in a dance of power. She raised her face toward the Wolf Moon and melded her voice with the wind. "Power!" a drum beat spoke. Brother Crow joined in, his boisterous calls reverberating in the night sky. Power! Power! I awoke to a drumbeat playing on the radio then sat on the edge of the couch running my fingers through my dampened hair. I stood, unsteady on my feet, and walked into the kitchen where I drank a glass of cold water and tried to analyze the dream. Power? Honor? Viviane had been trying to infuse strength into my spirit. Thinking of her dance I felt a burning sensation in my belly as if a swirling energy, a fire, glowed within me. I held my hand there and breathed deeply and the moonlight shining through the window called to me.

    I dressed warmly and crossed the threshold of my front door and stepped into the arctic night. Hard winter wrapped around me as I stared transfixed at the yellow globe hovering above the ice-silver night. Despite the cold I sat on the front step and listened to the night sounds of winter, so different from those of other seasons. I listened to the words of Mother Moon.

    This was the Craft of the Wise. It was listening to Mother Earth and to the moon's call. As women we have heard the moon's call from our origin but this is more than blind physical heeding. This was a conscious choice to acknowledge our ancient powers and to live a life of honor, dignity and creativity. This Craft was more than the wearing of black robes and enjoying the results of Magic. It was immersing oneself totally and fully into the deep wonder that was life. It was growing through the three stages of the female: maiden, mother, crone. When one has gained the knowledge of the maiden and the mother it is time to travel to the center of the web, to the stage of the crone. In today's world women often don't want to walk from the joys of the maiden and the mother. She has been taught that her value lies in her beauty, in her body. Approaching the door to the Crone can be terrifying, appalling but approach the door she must. She has the choice of remaining in the life of the maiden and mother until forced from it in humiliation and loneliness or she can journey through with head held high, with honor and dignity, with joyful anticipation. The elder women now learns from those still older than herself and she learns directly from the Source, from the Mother of All. She becomes the mentor of those in the first two stages. She is honored now as the circle is completed.

The moon seemed to pulsate as I watched her through the swaying trees' limbs which sounded in the wind like bones rattling. Her dark light soothed me. I stood and a feeling of gratefulness filled my heart. Something very old was teaching me. Oh, I knew the world would scoff that there is anything beyond what is seen, what is touched but I knew. *I knew.*

Inside again I set two logs upon the glowing embers and closed the wood stove's door. The waiting coals ignited the dry logs and the friendly crackling accompanied me as I prepared supper and listened to a recording of Mahler's Ninth Symphony. Cricket, Bess and Jake, their fur ruffled from a long sleep, sauntered sleepy-eyed into the kitchen at the first sounds of cooking.

The evening passed in pleasant solitude and when the hands on the clock came together at midnight I performed magic work for the new calendar year. I was coming to feel that I was joining the life of Wicca, was becoming a Woman of Power in this interval between Mother and Crone. This was my first cognizant act in this new life and as the aroma of patchouli rose up from the incense cone and blended with the flames of white candles I felt I was saying "yes" to Life Herself. Meditation filled me with peace and security. I thanked the universe for all my blessings and visualized the Light encompassing the globe, filling every heart that was heavy.

By one o'clock I had extinguished the candles, banked the fire, and gone to bed. My sleep was immediate and heavy and when the urgent voice cried out it became part of my dream. I felt drugged as the voice insisted and pulled me from sleep. Then I snapped awake, shoving the blankets aside and sitting on the edge of the bed, my heart pounding, waiting. The voice had warned me, "Wake up!"

I stood, and with only the cold light of the moon coming through the windows, I began to search, looking out the upstairs windows at first, then into each room. Was that voice only a part of a dream, I wondered? Maybe the cats had woken me by knocking something over. Quietly, I descended the stairs, pausing on each one to listen. The house seemed to inhale then hold its breath, waiting.

As I reached the kitchen I heard only the humming of the refrigerator and a thump from the wood stove as it cooled. Jake rubbed against my legs, delighted that this might mean a late night snack. He meowed plaintively and I laughed aloud at myself tiptoeing around the house in the middle of the night. He followed me as I walked to the window and looked up at the wintry white moon and the silhouette shadows of trees upon snow in the meadow. I heard Jake's claws scrambling on the linoleum and turned to see him running into the next room and thinking he wanted to play I called to him and followed.

It happened so quickly and what went through my frightened mind was, "He's desecrating my home!"

I knew who it was. I could smell him. The cloying stink of heavy aftershave filled my head as he grabbed me from behind, his arms tight around my neck and waist. His strength shocked me as I twisted, tried to pull his arm from my neck but he only tighten his grasp and hissed in my ear, "Where're your friends now?"

He wrestled me to the floor where he turned me on my stomach and with a knee on the small of my back, tied my hands together, then my feet. I grunted out a scream of outrage as he stood and looked down on me. How could this have happened? I had always assumed I could defend myself against an attack. My breath was caught in my throat and I struggled to inhale, my forehead on the cold linoleum, saliva puddling on the floor beneath my face. With a sobbing gasp I filled my lungs, then coughed. He bent down on one knee, checked the ropes and grunted. I'm gonna' stop you, you and your devilish friends."

My mind whirled trying to grab onto anything that was normal. I remembered an episode of the Oprah Winfrey show about self-defense in which the instructor advised not trying to reason with an attacker but to do everything physically possible to get attention from others while trying to get away. Both were pretty much out of the question here. What do I do now, Oprah? This is insane! I'm helpless with this madman and I'm talking to Oprah!

He pulled a chair up next to me and began to speak. "If only you hadn't kept on with your evil doings this wouldn't be happening to you." He frowned and slowly shook his head. "Don't you see that I have to get rid of each of you. This is the only way. Satan is in you, yes he is. He's got a tight hold on you, girl."

The terror rose in my as I listened and what was so horrendously frightening was that he sounded sane. He was calm, his voice soft as if he were trying to reason with *me*. I strained to look up at him. "You can't..." I began.

His calm broke as his face contorted in outrage. "*What*? I can't?" He snorted and leaned down to me, elbows on his knees. "I can do anything. Anything!"

I cringed from him. I knew that whatever I would say would set off his rage. I needed time. I needed to think clearly. He knelt beside me and began to pray, in a sing-song evangelistic frenzy.

"Jeee-susssss! We have here before us one who is in Satan's

clutches, one who does the devil's works. Hear me, Jeee-sussssss! You've led me here to save her eternal soul. You've given me power over her life, Lord. God Alll-miiighty, give me the strength to do your will. Satan is strroonnggg in these evil times. Saatannn is in our women, in our children. Women are weak, Lord, and have to be shown with a strrooonnnggg hand." He shook his fist and through gritted teeth his loud voice rose and fell as he ranted. "Let me cleanse this poor woman's soul, allow your servant to baptize her in blood, let me lead her from temp-taaation!"

He placed his hand on my head and I tried to scramble away from the invasion. The stench of his sweat, sour, thick and rancid filled my nostrils and my heart pounded like a machine, like it wasn't a part of me anymore. I managed to flip onto my back and scoot into a sitting position against the stove, staring at him like a cornered animal.

"You can't destroy everyone who doesn't agree with you," I croaked, furious at the weakness in my voice. Fear was causing me to shake, my teeth chattering as though I were freezing. I lowered my eyes under his glacial stare.

"It's not me. Don't you see? I have to do this. God wants it done." His voice growled low and condescending as he added, "Now...*how-can-I-disobey-God*?"

His words were chilling. Tears filled my eyes, rolled steadily down my cheeks and I tried to wipe them away with my shoulder, turning my face from him. Fear clutched me until I saw spots before my eyes, my stomach churned. Dizziness overcame me like something dark and heavy weighing me down and I felt as though I were falling into a tunnel. Helpless, so helpless lying on the floor beneath this psychotic fool. As I descended into the tunnel I could hear echoes of his crazed voice calling upon his Jeeee-susss.

Soft, warm light embraced me. Love was there. Was this death?

From this realm outside of what I knew, I saw myself on my kitchen floor, Leonard standing over me, his eyes rolled back in his head, perspiration dotting his forehead as he bellowed and thundered. I saw my body being kicked as he roared, "Saaataaannnn, leave. Saataaannn, be gone!"

As I sadly witnessed Leonard venting his fury upon that body I heard a voice and turned. Viviane was beside me. She wrapped her voluminous, black cloak around me and within that shelter I heard her say the Wiccan greeting, "Blessed be." Her husky voice was so welcomed, so soothing.

I leaned against her and whispered, "Am I dead?"

"Your fear has impelled you to leave your body but you still live, your body has breath."

"He's going to kill her," I said softly, as if that body on the floor was no longer mine.

"That need not be," she answered. "Where is your wisdom?"

I turned to her vacantly. "Wisdom?"

"Remember…" She reached up and touched my Third Eye and I heard Emily's voice say, "remember what they told us about being afraid. Remember the *Light*."

With those words, like a storybook opening page by page, I saw all that Walt and Grandmother had taught us, heard every loving word. Wrapped beside Viviane within her cloak I heard her say, "I am your wisdom. All that is within me is also within you. All that I know is all that the deepest part of you knows." She turned me to face her and smiled, "Now tell me, where is weakness where such strength lies?"

Time meant nothing when I returned to consciousness, tried to open my eyes and the pain of being in that battered body shot through me, causing me to cry out. Leonard was no longer beside me and I winced as I slowly pushed myself into a sitting position and listened. Blood dripped from my nose and covered the front of my pajamas. My eyes were nearly swollen shut and I gasped at the stabbing pain in my ribs but Viviane's words were in me and I was no longer paralyzed with fear. I breathed deeply through my mouth, concentrating on the Third Eye, focusing on my intent until I knew that I would not succumb to what Leonard had threatened. I felt the surge of power in my belly—the power, dignity and honor that Viviane had opened to me. I experienced centuries of female victimhood boil in me and the power in my belly knew the time of terror was ending.

The front door slammed and I heard his footsteps approaching. Still, there was no fear. A resolute conviction steadied me and I met his eyes when he entered the room. I could feel the cold air coming from his clothes. He stopped abruptly, met my gaze and frowned. He took two steps toward me menacingly then froze in mid-stride, confused.

"No, Leonard," I stated firmly through my swollen lips as I met his eyes.

"*What*? What did you say to me?" He laughed deep in his throat and advanced. "Look at you," he scoffed, "tied up like a calf about to be branded and you tell me 'No.' I do the telling around here, girlie, and you'd better know that right now. No female's going to tell *me* what I can or can't do." Dangerous things prowled in him.

He bent down and screamed into my face, "You hear me!"

Grabbing my shoulder he shook me while he pulled a cloth out of his jacket pocket. As he wound the cloth around his fist he said, "You're coming with me, girl. We're going somewhere where I'll have you on your knees praying."

His chuckle was cut short as I reached across the centuries, seized the ancient heritage within my bones and the power coursed through me. Like lava from a long-compressed volcano it struggled to the surface, bubbling and shattering years of suppression. Viviane's face was in my mind's eye, strong and calling up the blue light. Hundreds, thousands, millions of female faces swam before my eyes. Bruised faces, shamed faces, broken and blinded faces, burned faces. I saw the bent backs, the swollen bellies, necks broken in the noose, flesh blackened in the fires. I witnessed the women succumbing, women's childlike voices pleading, eyes vacant, souls deadened. I watched women trading bodies for bread, relinquishing their voice for safety. Mother Earth shed bitter tears as she felt the rape of females...the ripping of infant girlchildren, the ravage of the maiden, the mother, the crone.

"Strength!" Viviane's voice sang in my mind. "Honor! Dignity!"

The electric, crackling blue light shot out, intensified like a laser, called from my deepest consciousness, summoned from an ancient wellspring, claimed by the Witches, the shamans, the seers. It wavered, snakelike, in a circle, spinning around me from its huge reservoir of energy, knocking Leonard against the wall. Dazed, his face filled with a mixture of fury and fear, he cautiously approached me, lifted his arm to swing and as it neared the crackling light, sparks flew and he quickly drew back. His hollow eyes, narrowed to slits, searched my face as he held his burned hand against his chest.

"Witch!" he panted, trembling. He whirled around, grabbed a chair and, raising it over his head, roared out his rage as he hurled the chair toward me. It splintered and its pieces flew in every direction as if caught in a tornado.

The ropes from my wrists and ankles fell to the floor like coiled snakes. Rubbing his injured hand, his eyes slid from my face to the fallen ropes. Unsteadily, keeping my eyes on him, I stood and leaned against the stove, bent double against the pain. Hugging myself to ease the agony in my ribs I tried to focus on his face. He took a step forward, threateningly, then stopped, staring hard at me, fury filling his eyes. He quoted the bible through gritted teeth: "Therefore shall her plagues come in one day, death, and mourning, and famine; and she shall be utterly burned with fire: for strong is the Lord God who judges her."

He backed away slowly then turned and ran. I stood alone in the kitchen and heard the engine of his car start and the squeal of tires as he sped away.

I sighed heavily and the blue light crackled and vanished, leaving in its wake the faint aroma of burning incense, trailing clouds of glory. Feeling like I had just awakened from a nightmare I shut the door then sank into the chair beside me, exhausted, stupefied.

The dark day outside was sheathed in ice. Wind wailed like wolves through the forest beyond the meadow. I looked at the ropes on the floor, amazed at the frayed strands. Staring into space I recalled Viviane's words: "I am your wisdom." All along, it had been there. All these sad, battered centuries...waiting. Like the fallen princess in the fairy tales waiting for the kiss of the prince upon her forehead but no, not the prince but the kiss of Source upon her brow.

Shelly found me later, as night was approaching. The phone lines had been cut and I knew I couldn't drive with the pain I was experiencing so I took a long, hot shower and lay down. My cats joined me, lying close to me, kneading the blankets, licking my hands and face as if trying to console me. I concentrated on sending a message to Shelly, asking her to come to me. I had fallen into a deep sleep when I heard her voice.

"Diana?" She was kneeling by my bed, holding my hand. "God...Diana, wake up!"

I opened my eyes and squeezed her hand, whispering, "Good. You're here."

"What happened?" Her eyes were filled with tears.

"Leonard..."

"That bastard! *He* did this to you?"

I shook my head and said, "Listen...listen. I want to tell you..."

"Did you call the police? No, you couldn't have, the lines are dead." She stood and began pacing the room. "I'm taking you to the hospital. Can you walk?" She started to pull the covers from me and I kept shaking my head.

"Shelly! Listen to me." It was so hard speak through swollen lips I was becoming exasperated. *"Listen!"*

She stopped and stared at me and from her eyes I knew I looked terrible. Tears fell and she began sobbing. "Oh, Diana..." She lay her head beside me on the pillow while she held me and cried.

"I need you to do something for me, Shelly."

She sat up, held my hand and answered, "What? What do you need?"

"I want you to get to a phone, call everyone and tell them to come here. It's very important that everyone come. Don't go to the police. Understand?"

She nodded. "You'll be okay alone? Why won't you let me take you to the hospital? I can't leave you here! What if he comes back?" Her eyes were huge in her panic.

"He's not coming back."

"But..."

"Shelly."

She nodded again. "Well, if you're sure. Can I get you anything before I leave?"

"First turn the heat up. I'm freezing. And make some chamomile tea for me." I smiled to try to reassure her. "You know where I keep everything."

She returned with the tea and helped me sit up with pillows propped behind me. She straightened my blankets, turned the light on by my bed, fussed some more then finally left to make the calls. I had to tell everyone what had happened. I had to let them know what I had learned.

I awoke much later to the sounds of their voices as they ascended the stairs to my bedroom. They circled my bed, whispering, their faces sad and concerned.

I sat up and managed a short laugh. "I'm not dead, for heaven's sake," I croaked.

"You look like hell," Don said. They laughed uncomfortably and began to find places to sit. Emily took my hand and carefully curled up next to me on the bed. She looked into my eyes with deep understanding, a little smile at the corners of her lips. "You know, don't you, Emily?"

She patted my cheek and said, "Grandmother knew what was going to happen. She told me not to be scared."

"Tell us," George said as he sat on the edge of the bed.

I quietly told them a short version of my ordeal with Leonard. The men's faces contorted with anger until I told them to set aside judgment until I was finished. I told them everything and the room was quiet.

"That's what Walt was trying to tell us that day on the bridge. Remember?" Jeff's eyes searched each face. "He told us about the path of fear, about seeing ourselves as victims, about anger and violence. He said we have power in our own lives because we are part of the Creator."

George finished Jeff's words by quoting those startling words Walt had told us that when we know that we are God we will be incapable of fear.

They turned to me and Jeff asked, "Is that what you realized?"

"When it first happened, when he grabbed me I reacted like anyone would. I panicked and all my strength left me, I felt nauseous, saw spots before my eyes. All these physical symptoms were immediate."

Dorothy shook her head and added, "And people don't believe that emotions cause illness."

I nodded in agreement and continued. "I felt like a helpless victim and became so terrified that I lost consciousness. When Viviane reminded me to remember the Light, when she told me of my wisdom and I returned to my body the fear was completely gone. I knew I had the power to control my own life and along with that feeling of power I felt compassion for Leonard, an understanding of what drove him. I knew it was true what Walt told us—that he would eventually find his way, as will everyone. I knew that each person's divine destiny is to realize Who they are."

"So it's all true," Jeff said softly, "even this. Everything they told us about ourselves. It's real."

"It's real," I answered with a tired sigh.

"You don't feel you ought to go to the police?" Robert asked.

I shook my head. "It's over. Don't you see that he can't hurt any of us? What Walt told us, what I've experienced is true for *everyone*. This is why I called you all here. He may try to hurt you but, knowing what I just told you, he can't succeed."

"And you don't want to go to the hospital? He hurt you, Diana. You may have internal injuries." Shelly took my hands in hers, imploring me with her eyes. "Really, you ought to go."

"Don't you *get it*?" I asked, rising against the pillows despite the pain in my ribs. "If everything they told us is real, if all our power is within, if emotions make the body sick then can't we *heal* ourselves as well?"

Their faces were blank so I continued. "There are times when we need outside help, doctors, surgeons but that's because we're not yet far enough along in our evolution to heal everything. I think that someday we'll have that ability but right now we sometimes need help from others. I feel, no...I *know*, that I can heal myself. There is this power within. It can't be limited, can it? I mean, if it can put a barrier of light around me to protect me from Leonard's attack then why can't it heal me?"

George touched me and chuckled. "We humans can be so dense, can't we? Look what it took for you to know that what Walt told us was literal truth! We have to be pushed up against the wall before anything sinks in. Remember that old adage that there are no atheists in foxholes? It seems we have to face death before we reach out, or reach in."

"We're always placing limits on ourselves, aren't we? You're right, Diana. We've seen miracles, wonders beyond imagination. The power of Creation has no limits." Robert carefully bent over me and kissed me on the cheek.

"Let *us* help," Emily suggested. "We can do a circle around you. We'll pretend we're in the woods around the fire like we were with Grandmother and Walt." Her eyes were eager at the thought of helping, of creating something beautiful. "And let's bless Leonard so that he can find the Light and learn how to love."

Let's bless Leonard? Only Emily had that insight but we all knew what she meant.

"What a great idea, Emily," Don agreed. He was seated on a small rocking chair in the corner of the room, his long legs awkwardly drawn up to his chest. He stood and addressed Emily, "What do you think we should do?"

She began, "Let's get candles and that can be like the fire in the woods."

"We can do the smudging ceremony that Robert showed us," Dorothy suggested. "Do you have any sage or incense?"

One of my kitchen cabinets contained glass jars filled with all the various herbs from last year's garden. They were clearly labeled and I told her where to find them. She and Don left the room and returned shortly with candles, the jar of dried sage, matches and a small crockery bowl. I knew that all these material things were not necessary for healing but, instead, offered us the sensory means to transport us to a state of mind or awareness of our power.

A light snowfall had begun outside the windows and the sky had darkened. The dimness within the bedroom vanished as the candles were lighted, faces taking on the glow from the flames. Robert unscrewed the lid of the jar, took out two sprigs of sage and lay them in the bowl. Everyone gathered around the bed as he lit the edge of one leaf and softly blew on the tiny flame. The flame died out and the sage began to send up its familiar fragrant smoke. He cupped his hand around the swirling spirals and, with closed eyes, drew the smoke over his head and down to his heart then passed the bowl to Don. When the bowl, warm from its smoldering contents, was handed to me, I drew the smoke over the top part of my body and Shelly assisted by smudging me from my waist down. She set the bowl on my nightstand and everyone held hands.

I closed my eyes, focused within and soon felt the pulsing between my eyebrows. Shelly's beautiful voice began chanting and the others joined until the combination of sounds began to resonate within me, a harmony of healing. I heard Grandmother's voice, Walt's voice within me encouraging, affirming. My awareness went inside into my blood, bones, tissues until the very DNA, the codes of me were awakened and ignited to follow an ancient pattern.

From this deep place I felt heat and movement. My entire body was pulsating, humming with sounds that became solid, sounds that were before there were words, sounds that caused the magnificent order. This synchronized dance of molecules and atoms received from the original, unlimited Source.

After a timeless expanse the sounds of chanting softened and the sensation of movement within me subsided. I opened my eyes to the astounded faces of my friends surrounding me. I touched my chest, my face then sat up and slowly swung my legs over the side of the bed. I stood and ran my hands down over my body.

I felt like shouting to the world, "It's begun!" Oh, that everyone could know.

Within me I heard the words of Whitman:

> *I celebrate myself, and sing myself,*
> *And what I assume you shall assume,*
> *For every atom belonging to me as good belongs to you...*
> *I sing the body electric...*
> *I sing the body electric!*

Chapter 11

The Celebration

From our plaintive natal cries we travel to the dark night's illumination. Shapeshifters walk from the shadows of fog, from the shadows of shadows. Within the brain-nest the eye blinks. The singing of the whales is in harmony with the drumming of our hearts. The songlines of First Nations surround our humming universe. See the star maps and orient yourself in this time that will bind us together. Come, my friends, the celebration begins.

Theodore Roethke once wrote, "In a dark time, the eye begins to see." On that first night of the new year I experienced what had lain fallow within me. In that dark time I saw. I *knew*. We are not helpless creatures in a chaotic world. We are marvels!

The months that followed were quiet, snow-filled and contemplative flowing like the ocean's currents. No matter how much verbal preparation one has, a complete change of identity leaves a gap that must be filled. In those reflective days my friends and I grew into our new Selves. Our daily lives were a metamorphosis in a chrysalis from which we would emerge, new beings capable of spiritual flight.

Brother Crow had become my constant companion and I'd spot him flying overhead or perched in the trees calling out to me in his raucous voice. His habit of bringing gifts to me was a delight and every day I would find his gleanings left in my window box that he, evidently, considered wonderful: feathers, shells, sea glass, little puffs of animal fur, a key, bits of foil, tinsel, one small mitten and other bits of spangles and frippery. I loved the sight of his iridescent plumage as he followed me on my walks, sometimes strutting beside me, at other times flying from tree to tree and often hitchhiking upon my shoulder.

Shelly shared Thoreau's thoughts on crows with me. She was reading a book of his journals in which on March 23, 1856, he had written: "This bird sees the white man come and the Indian withdraw, but it withdraws not. Its untamed voice is still heard above the tinkling of the forge...it remains to remind us of aboriginal nature."

As winter progressed, daylight lingered and the thaw descended deep into the earth. Snowstorms changed to icy rains then warmed into spring showers. Buds grew plump on trees and promised that soon a watercolor wash of green would begin to appear. The air was heavy with the aroma of earth warming under the returning sun and the long winter's silence was broken as birds' songs began to fill the mornings. I shed my woolen clothes and boots and delighted in the freedom of feeling soothing sunlight upon my skin. Spring was here. Nature was reborn.

As I worked in my gardens, clearing the debris that had accumulated over the winter and pulling up remnants of last autumn's annuals, I felt the current of life within the rich soil. I dug into the cool, moist earth and it seemed to hum with vitality. Whitman wrote of this: "Underneath, the divine soil. Overhead, the sun." The divine soil was readying itself to receive the seeds and to prosper. The sun was hot on my back as I knelt in my herb garden picking dead leaves away from the new green growth, careful not to disturb the delicate crocus, which sprang up everywhere.

I laughed as Jake rolled on his back by the thick stalks of faded lavender, a contented cat smile on his face. I rubbed his fat, orange furry belly and he kicked my hand with his back feet in mock ferociousness before changing his mind and shoving his head under my hand for a nice scratch. Cricket was lying stretched out to his full length in the sunlight by the dried catnip plants like a sated tick, eyes half-closed in delight and my little Bess was curled up among the dense ground-cover, almost hidden. Cats know how to feed their souls, how to live the Zen life.

This idyllic scene was disrupted when Brother Crow, with a frantic flapping of wings, swooped from the sky barely missing Cricket who leaped from his slumber and gazed up at Crow perched in the apple tree. Crow raised his black head and cawed boisterous laughter. Cricket, embarrassed, glanced at me then, with slow cat dignity began to wash his foot as if this were the real reason he woke up. Yeah, sometimes you can be in a deep sleep and something prods at you to do something about that dirty foot. Being King Cat in the neighborhood was a heavy burden he carried and was always on guard to protect his reputation.

Clouds began gathering and the sun I had enjoyed all morning kept fading in and out. The air was heavy with the rain to come. After returning the gardening tools to the shed I went to the clothesline in the back yard where, earlier that morning, I had hung sheets to dry in the April wind. As I unclipped the clothespins holding them onto the line I gathered the sheets to me and inhaled their fresh spring aroma. They smelled like Walt. Oh, I missed him. I missed his deep, gentle voice, his twinkling eyes, his strength, his companionship. And Grandmother...I wished she lived just down the road so I could visit her whenever I wanted, sit by her side and bathe in her wisdom and mischievous humor. I daily burned a type of incense that reminded me of her: apples, cinnamon and sandalwood. I was homesick for my elder friends.

It had been months since we had seen our teachers. Each time we enjoyed a ceremonial circle we anticipated their arrival—full moons, Imbolc on February first and the Vernal Equinox of March twenty-first on which we celebrated the time of year when the nights and days are equal in hours. Again, the balance. The next celebration was to be Beltane on May 1, the day when the ancient custom of reveling in Nature's rebirth is observed.

As I walked into the house, tripping on cats and trailing sheets I anticipated a pleasant afternoon of writing overdue letters, reading a book I was eager to get back to and writing in my journal. I had put in a full week in my studio and was current on all my deadlines so an afternoon of freedom was pleasurable.

I lit a fire in the wood stove to take away the chill, made a cup of coffee and sat in the chair by the fire with my journal. These notebooks of my journey with Walt and Grandmother were piling up. This was my sixth one and I wondered how many more there would be, how long our teachers would continue to be in our lives and what other wonders they intended to show us. I uncapped my pen, shifted the notebook on my lap and began to write.

Deep in concentration, my pen hurried across the lines, page after page. A flash of light caused me to jump, the ink trailing a line across the page and when I looked up Grandmother was sitting in the chair opposite me. She looked smaller than usual in the big wingback chair, her hands folded primly on her lap, her tiny moccasined feet crossed. I jumped to my feet, the notebook falling to the floor.

"Grandmother!" I gasped, noticing the air was heavy with her mysterious, spicy scent.

"You be feeling like visiting Grandmother, hmmm?" she asked in a teasing voice.

"Grandmother!" I repeated as I stood above her with my mouth opened.

Her laughter shook her entire body and she slapped her knees and, between giggles, said, "Ohhh, Diana, you be so funny. You look like you be so scared of poor old Grandmother."

I reached down to hug her and explained, "Not scared. You know that." I kissed her wrinkled cheek and added, "Surprised. You startled me so." I sat down, reached out and took her tiny hands in mine. "Oh, I've been missing you."

"Grandmother be knowing that," she crooned, squeezing my hands.

"But I never thought I'd see you here in my house." I gazed lovingly at her, thrilled at her presence.

"Why not here? Why not house?" she asked. "Grandmother be with you in all times. You not know that by now?"

"Let me get you something...a cup of coffee or tea?" I was as giddy as a girl, playing hostess to this most beloved woman.

"That be nice. Hot cup of tea while we have talk."

She followed me into the kitchen where I lit the burner under the kettle and watched her as she gazed around the room.

"You make home nice. You bring nature inside," she said, walking around and touching the dried herbs hanging, the crystals and rocks on the windowsill, the plants. Jake, hearing Grandmother's voice had come to investigate. He regally entered the kitchen, stretched luxuriously with a wide, toothy yawn and began rubbing against her legs.

We took our cups into the living room and sat again by the fire. Holding the cup balanced on one knee she reached down and picked up my notebook from where I'd dropped it on the floor by her chair. Tapping her finger on its cover, she asked gently, "You still be writing story of Grandmother and Walt? You be making all the words and telling everything?"

I reached out for the book and when she handed it to me I hugged it protectively to my chest, explaining, "Since the first day. I'm glad that no one but me will ever read this. If anyone ever got hold of this…"

"Why you be writing all this?" she inquired.

Concerned that I had offended her, I said quickly, "When I first met Walt I thought I was going crazy. Then you came! It was all so insane that I started writing as a sort of therapy. Then...well, then I just continued because I never wanted to forget anything about you and Walt or anything you'd ever said to us."

"Oh, you not forget." She lifted her tea cup as Jake jumped onto her lap, turning circles as he made a sleeping nest.

I laughed and answered, "You're right. How could I forget one detail?"

"But there be more," she confided in a whisper.

"More? You mean more to the story?"

"That be true but I mean there be more reason why you be writing."

I waited, looking at her expectantly. Her face was very earnest, her smoky eyes burning deep into mine. A feeling began to stir in me, a glimmer of what she meant.

"Oh, no, Grandmother." I stared at her then began to laugh nervously. I placed the notebook on the little table between us, trying to distance myself from what she was requesting. "I think I know what you're getting at."

She bent forward and poked the notebook with one finger, frowning. "Grandmother be getting at this: notebooks gonna' become book, book going to go out to all people."

"You're talking about this becoming a published book?" I cried, half rising from my chair.

She nodded calmly. "That what Grandmother be talking about."

"But that can't be!" I argued. "Remember? You said that we are not to try to convince anyone about the Light. You said that the Light would touch others, not us. You…"

"That be true."

"Then how…"

She shook her head in frustration. "Diana, *you* not going to go out making people listen to you. *Book* be going out."

"But it's the same thing!" I argued, my face flushing. "If I write it then it's my story and if it's in a book isn't that me trying to persuade others to believe as I do?"

"You not be trying to persuade anyone about any thing. You be telling story. You not *make* people buy book. You not *make* anyone read it. They make *choice* to read it. Maybe it make them feel good. Maybe they begin to think they be part of God and Goddess too and maybe they think it be big bunch of silliness. That be okay too." She smiled and added tenderly, "This be new path for you."

"What do you mean?"

"New path. You be saying all along that you not happy with work you do. You not like to do advertising stuff anymore, hmmm? Remember when Grandmother be telling you that there be better way for you, there be way that make heart full?"

I nodded.

"This be way," she said after a moment.

"A book," I said quietly. Only in my most private dreams had I thought of being a writer. It had always seemed like something for others, not for me. I felt a tingle of excitement at the thought that this could be. "But how…"

"You not be starting that worry stuff now," she interrupted, making a gesture of dismissal. "You not be worrying about anything. You just be starting to put all those words into that computer thing you use. Words come one after another and soon you have it all down for book. Oh, it be lots of work but that be okay because it be loving work. Anything anyone do with love not be really work."

"And it's okay to...ah...make money on this?" I floundered. "It doesn't seem right to…"

She cut me off, saying, "Baaaa! Why people think it be bad to make money on something they love doing? Why people think only way they should take money is from doing job they hate? Why you think money be bad?"

"It just seems that…" I was so confused.

"Some people think money be bad," she said more gently. "That not be truth. You be hurting someone to get money, that be bad. You steal from them, that bad. You greedy, that be bad. You think money be more important than people, that be bad too. Money just be symbol. Instead of trading *things* you have money to trade. It be how you get things you need to live and enjoy. You get money to buy food, warm house, warm clothes. You buy pretty things," she pointed at the candles, the plants and the paintings on the walls. "That be nice too but you live in simple way and you know that even if you not have lots of pretty things you still be happy. You not spend all day, all life getting so much money you never be able to use it. You not see *money as power* 'cause you know that true power be within." She pressed her hand against her chest. "You see difference, hmmm. You use money for need...not for greed."

"Thank you, Grandmother," I sighed in relief. "This is such a gift." I recalled the words Walt had said to me while we sat on the pier in Plymouth: "Where is your heart? Where do you wander in your dreams? Where do you lose yourself and merge with that which is greater?" I had answered, "Art, writing."

In my head I began to weave my story, make lace with words. I felt a longing to create a book that would feel green, that would smell of grass and forests. A book that would magically breathe in the night-hours and hold starlight between its pages.

Grandmother picked up her cup of tea and sipped daintily. "Writing be your gift. You have storytelling in blood. You tell people they be so wonderful, that they be miracles. You tell people all that stuff in book. Now," she pointed at my notebook, "you read to Grandmother."

And during that rainy afternoon by the firelight Grandmother and I shared the story.

Early spring days led into that wondrous time when forsythia poured its golden fountains over the emerald grass. A row of double-bloom forsythia along the meadow took my breath away in its luxurious beauty. Once the forsythia bloomed I knew the daffodil would soon follow and one morning as I returned home after my Saturday morning errands, after the sun had warmed the gardens, I was startled at the seemingly sudden opening of hundreds of daffodils along the flagstone path leading to my front steps and there, in the meadows and under the trees those delightful yellow harbingers of spring were nodding in the gentle breeze. Hyacinth's fleshy, fragrant heads were bent to the ground with their own weight, not fully opened yet but hints of their pink, blue, white color peeking through. The tulips, also, would be showing their satin-bright colors soon, their tight buds still green, hiding the glory that they would be displaying.

Can anything be more magical than springtime? From the frozen, barren ground comes this rebirth, this reawakening, this yearly miracle! It was almost more than I could comprehend as I walked around my yard, touching branches, delicate petals, kneeling on the ground to saturate my senses with the various scents. The dogwood's branches were opulent with the white and pink buds, fat bumblebees languidly thirsting at every one. The lilac bushes were fuller than I had ever seen them, massive lush spires of purple and white buds almost straining their seams, eager to send out their intoxicating fragrance. It's as though Nature, held back for so many months, was sending out fireworks, a triumphant parade of life.

I picked bouquets for my home and once inside, my eyes adjusting to the absence of that brilliant sunlight, created displays around the freshly cleaned rooms. After making a pot of coffee, I raised several windows to welcome in the late April air. A knock at the door sent me to greet whoever was there. Shelly stood on my front step, a small white box tied with string in her hands. I opened the door wide and hugged her.

"Hi!" she smiled, her pale blue eyes sparkling in happiness. "Isn't this the best spring ever? Your yard looks like a fairyland," she bubbled, as she handed me the box. "Goodies from the Morning Glory bakery. Yum."

"I must have known you were coming. I just made a pot of coffee," I chatted, taking the box from her as we walked into the kitchen. "Let's set up a tray and sit at the picnic table. I just can't bear to miss any of this sunshine."

Outside, seated at the picnic table, we moaned and groaned over the apricot Danish she had brought. "The best!" I said, smacking my lips and licking my fingers. "I feel like I'm stoned this tastes so good."

"I feel like that all the time now," Shelly laughed. "Really. I can understand why people want to take drugs if it feels like this."

"Drugs can't compare, can they? There's a big down side, or shadowside, as Grandmother calls it, to drugs. People get caught in that awful spiral of needing them, getting them, using them, needing them again. Lives are wrecked, to mention nothing of health. But," I agreed, "it does feel like I'm high all the time."

After we finished every crumb in that box, we wandered around my yard then along the dirt road, which twisted for about two miles before coming to a paved road. We talked, as we slowly meandered, of our "life's work." Her pottery was selling well in shops all over New England and she had even gotten orders from California and Washington. Her classes at the massage therapy school were going well and she would receive her degree in less than a year. She was thinking of quitting her night job at the coffee shop and devoting more time to pottery.

"I guess it's time to take that 'leap' Grandmother told us about." We laughed at Grandmother's words that day: "It be like jumping out of plane. It be scary at first but then you find you always safe and pretty soon you jumping all the time and it be fun!"

Shelly already knew about Grandmother's visit for I had called her the next day and related the story and my dismay and excitement at transforming my journals into a book. "It's coming along," I told her when she inquired, "but it's certainly not an easy process making anything that reads like a book from my journals."

"She said it wasn't going to be easy," I laughed, then quoted her, "It not be easy."

"But it be fun," Shelly added.

I nodded, smiling at the thoughts of my dear old teacher. "Yeah, it be fun," I agreed.

Like Shelly, I was contemplating making that leap, leaving the security of a known means of income, trusting that the new venture would supply my needs. If I didn't take on any new clients the commitments to those I had would be completed in about a month. If I lived very frugally and worked daily on the book I could live on what I had squirreled away in my savings account. I may even be able to take out a small home equity loan to get me through a year without working in my studio. Grandmother was right. It was very much like making a leap and it was scary and in a strange kind of way it was even fun.

Spring's display continued and in a few days we'd be celebrating May 1, Beltane. Everyone gathered at my house to make plans for this day. It was a clear, warm night and the peepers in the woods were chorusing their joy that mating time was here. Robert had brought huge bouquets from his gardens and, looking around at the filled vases in every room, asked if I would mind if he gave them to Shelly who had no space at her apartment to garden. Shelly was delighted and, in turn, shared them with George, Jeff, Don and Dorothy. Then everyone walked out into the night to pick from my gardens, laughing and sharing under the moon's illumination. Later, I carefully wrapped their bouquets in wet paper towels surrounded by plastic bags which were held tightly by rubber bands around the stems. The kitchen looked like a florist's shop with flowers lying all over the countertop.

Over coffee and more of those wonderful pastries from Shelly we made our plans for Beltane, the following Saturday. Robert, Dorothy and Emily were in charge of creating a Maypole and finding a book at the library on how to do that intricate, weaving Maypole dance. Robert would accompany our dance with his drum. We would have the ceremonial fire in the same place in the woods and dress in festive, flowing costumes, weather permitting. Next came the important task of selecting the menu and after much discussion selected simple things that would not require anyone having to stay inside and cook on that day: salads, fruit, fresh breads, cheeses, pastries.

Friday night I listened to the weather forecast, relieved and delighted that this warm, clear spell would continue and Saturday morning I awoke to bright sunshine beginning to peek over the treetops. When I opened my front door to allow three kitties out, the warmth greeted me, even at this early hour. As I walked out onto the cool, green lawn heavily laden with diamond dewdrops, the grass released its scent under my bare feet. I listened to the morning's symphony of birds, finding it almost impossible to believe that a few months earlier that same place was a frozen wasteland. Following the sound I strolled down the grassy incline that led to the herb gardens from where I could see the bird feeders hanging from the trees near the meadow. I made a mental note to go to the feed and grain store to buy another fifty pounds of seed. Over the winter months with eleven feeders to fill I would go through fifty pounds in a week but with the warming weather that amount would last a month. I could hear Brother Crow and his clan in the distance awakening the world with their harsh cries. The last gift he had left me was a set of keys—whole set on a ring. Now, where, do you suppose, did he steal that?

Later that morning, as I was in the kitchen cutting fruit I heard car doors slam and my friends walked through the open front door with happy greetings. I wiped my hands on a towel and went to greet them, laughing and exclaiming over their wonderful outfits. Everyone had certainly given thought to the meaning of this day as they displayed their fine array like peacocks. Crowns of flowers, laurel, feathers and lace adorned every head and brightly colored shirts, pants, flowing skirts and scarves, and jeweled and feathered masks made my kitchen look like Mardi Gras. Emily and Dorothy were the most resplendent in green leotards and tights with pastel scarves around their waists arranged like skirts, apple blossom crowns upon their heads and their faces painted in green, sparkling leaf designs. On each brow, between the eyes was drawn the blue triple-Goddess design that we had seen on Viviane.

Dorothy had brought her face paints, set them up on the kitchen table and began to paint everyone's face: flowers, stars, hearts but always the triple-Goddess on the forehead. This enhanced my outfit of a black leotard and a long, silky black skirt on which I had painted silver pentagrams. A crown of lavender and rosemary upon my head made me feel like a maiden rather than one who was approaching her crone years.

I don't know where George dug up his outfit but he looked like someone who had wandered off Haight & Ashbury Streets in the heyday of the Flower Children.

He gave me a peace sign salute and chuckled, "Peace 'n love, sister."

"I wouldn't wear that outfit in public, George. You look like you got dressed under the influence of LSD," I giggled.

He looked down at his flowered shirt, pink bell-bottoms and bright green flip-flops and, brushing imaginary lint from his cuffs, answered haughtily, "Jealousy." He walked away, his head held high, swinging the beads around his neck with one finger.

Robert, Emily and Dorothy left to go into the meadow and erect the Maypole, being very mysterious and refusing any help. Bags were brought in and emptied of their contents: food, candles, ribbons, wind chimes, incense, crystals and anything magical and beautiful that people wanted to include in our ceremony. We prepared lunch and stored it in the refrigerator for later then sat at the kitchen table drinking coffee and tea and discussing our plans for the day.

"Mama and Robert said we can go see the Maypole," Emily shouted as she burst excitedly through the front door, seeming like a tiny wood sprite as she motioned for us to follow her. There, in the middle of the green grass of the meadow stood the Maypole, appearing foreign and exotic with its myriad colored streamers flowing from the top of the tall pole and trailing to the grass below, undulating gently in the breeze.

After Dorothy told us about the dance and rhythm and how it was to be done in order to eventually wind the ribbons together in a pattern down the pole, Robert began to beat the drum. Laughing, tripping, often going in the wrong direction, the dance started to take form. Finally, under Dorothy's hilarious instructions, we got the hang of it and, barefoot and flowing, saw the tapestry of ribbons slowly winding together. When there was no longer enough length on the streamers to hold onto and duck under we lay, tired and happy on the grass, surveying the outcome of our boisterous Maypole dance.

"Oh, that was fun," yelled Emily, "let's do it again!"

Everyone over five years of age groaned and begged Emily to let us just lay on the grass and recuperate. As we lay in that emerald green meadow in the golden sunlight we heard the faint, breathy sounds of Grandmother's flute.

"It's Grandmother!" Emily exclaimed, jumping up from the ground and looking all around. Everyone waited and from the edge of the meadow by the woods we saw them. We raced to greet them and as I stood within the warm circle of Walt's arms smelling his sweet scent of hay fields, herbs, and April wind it was as though I were holding Mother Earth Herself. There we were in their radiant glow, protected and loved.

"Oh, Walt, I've missed you," I crooned, lying my head on his big chest.

Grandmother peered at me, then at Walt and said, "Maybe she think you go off somewhere on big vacation. Maybe she think you go hibernate like some big ol' bear."

Walt played along with her and said innocently, "But I didn't go anyplace. Maybe she couldn't see me because she needs glasses. What do you think, Grandmother?"

She hunched her shoulders and folded her arms, looking like she was deep in thought, "Hmmm. Maybe that be so. Maybe we have tough time making this one finally see Light."

I giggled at the thought of the Creator prescribing eyewear for me and kissed him, his soft white beard, tickling my nose. Then I stepped back so that others could greet him, observing the affect he had on everyone. The old Sage touched and laughed and caressed, spreading a glow around us that was visible. They sat on the green grass and we circled them like chicks finding comfort within the feathered safety of their mother. Emily ran to the edge of the meadow, returning shortly with two daffodils, handing them solemnly to Walt and Grandmother. They smiled their thanks and tucked the flowers behind their ears, adding to their beauty.

Both were dressed today entirely in white. The white leather of Grandmother's tunic and pants was as soft as velvet and her tiny moccasins were beaded in rainbow colors. Around her neck hung strands of shells and beads and silver. Contrasting with her clothes, her dark skin seemed darker, richer. Walt was barefoot and his trousers and loose blouse were of a thinly woven linen. The wide-brimmed hat, tilted, as always, over one shaded eye, seemed like a crown over his thick, white hair and beard. Our teachers glowed in the sunlight. A Wordsworth poem came to my mind:

> *There was a time, when meadow, grove and stream,*
> *The earth, and every common sight,*
> *To me did seem appareled in celestial light.*
> *The glory and the freshness of a dream.*

Grandmother welcomed Jake onto her lap. He smiled up at her and licked her fingers, purring in ecstasy. "Time to talk today of many things," she began. "Time be here to prepare you."

Prepare us? What now! Time out!

She glanced at me and frowned and I remained silent. "You come long way on path. You learn many things. Diana go through dark time with Leonard and she learn that Walt and Grandmother speak truth when they say power be within. You learn you have power to heal selves. You know now you never again have to shrink at shadows, hmmm?"

Her eyes turned to me like lasers and she asked, "You know why you go through dark time with Leonard?"

I looked around at my companions as if they had the answer, then said, "He wanted to stop us. He…"

She shook her head and said, "It not have anything to do with what *he* want. Think!"

I shrugged my shoulders, feeling a bit embarrassed. "Was it some sort of test?"

"Test?" She looked around, "Somebody around here passing out tests? What test you be talking about?" Her face softened and her eyes encouraged me.

"Well," I began, flustered, "stopping Leonard from killing me, for heaven's sake."

"Oh," she said, making a dismissive gesture, "that not be test. That be stuff *you* make."

"*Me?*"

She nodded emphatically. "That be right. We tell you Light be in you. We give you all lessons but you not really believe 'til you prove it to self." She peered at me, reminding me of Brother Crow's scrutiny. "It not be test. It be gift you give self."

"Gift? Some gift!" I muttered in a huff.

"That be right. *Gift*," she stated emphatically. "You be using Leonard's anger to see Light but that be okay. That be what most people be doing. They find all kind of troubles so they can solve them, and grow and finally see that they be God."

I pondered her words, then asked, "So life doesn't have to be so hard? It's just that we can't believe Who we really are?"

She smiled and nodded. "That be right. Not have to be so hard."

Her smile soothed me and I said softly, "You're so patient with us,

Grandmother."

"That's 'cause Grandmother loves you," she confided, covering my hand with hers.

I smiled inwardly at her way of speaking, loving how simple her words were, yet so wise. "Will others begin to know these things…" my eyes searched her face, Walt's face. "…the others who are being touched by the Light?"

"All will eventually know," Walt began, "for that is the Light's purpose—to enlighten." He raised his arms, his eyes peaceful, as he looked upon us. "The Light opens to you your planet's, your race's drama. Often your minds cannot grasp the limitlessness of the universe, galaxies without end. Your minds cannot conceive what the Spirit truly is for that is beyond mind.

"Know this," he touched Shelly who sat next to him. "Even in the incomprehensible vastness, each individual holds the hidden buds of all life. Every one has a place, a purpose, is an integral part of the limitlessness. When a thirsty tree is given water does not every part benefit? Does not the water, as it seeps into the roots, continuing upward, unseen, nourish every bud and leaf? In your world-minds you separate from the water of creation and that causes you to feel cut off, alone and powerless in such a vast mystery."

Emily, drowsy from the morning's activity, rolled to where Walt sat and, like Jake sleeping in the nest of Grandmother's lap, curled up on his crossed legs, her eyes slowly closing. He ran his fingers through her tangled curls and his voice softened so as not to awaken her. "Do you not see, my friends, that life builds upon life? Humankind has always and will always be called by a silent Voice to create. Every living thing struggles to become and this struggle opens Divinity. From your beginning you have come to this time and this time offers the choice. People can continue in tears and struggle or they can make the leap as one stepping from the confinement of armor, to tread lightly and freely. What people have carried as their armor has imprisoned them."

Jeff gave Walt a curious look and asked, "What's the armor, Walt?"

He gently lifted Emily slightly and shifted position before answering. "The armor, Jeff, is all that you pull tight around yourselves for protection. In your armor you cut yourself off from the Light and live in slavery. Armor is grasping and hurting others to gain things of the world. It is seeing power in the financial, political, military world. This puts you in the life-battle, that fight to gain and to keep power over others. It imprisons you within it and shuts out Spirit.

"Armor is racism which you think will protect you from others who are seemingly different. Armor is shutting out love to protect yourself from hurt." He draped his arm over Jeff's shoulder and added, "The Light is here but the choice is yours."

A choice? Does it all comes down to *our* choice, *our* decision to continue living in the craziness and violence or to finally realize Who we are? Nothing is preordained. There are possibilities but haven't there always been possibilities and throughout history so often the human heart has chosen hate over love, war over peace. God help us.

Grandmother knew my thoughts and said somberly while she scratched Jake's head, "Light come to encourage, to help people to receive."

"You see, my friends," Walt began telling us, "humanity must awaken from its hypnotic ways. People have hypnotized themselves into believing that power lies in Wall Street, in banks, in bombs, in jobs. As long as humanity continues this mad illusion wars will continue, poverty will continue, hunger, loneliness, crime, drug addiction, child abuse, homelessness, racism—all will continue until humanity can endure it no more and looks beyond the human scene to the Spirit, to the Light. When everyone begins to realize that God,

Goddess lives in every individual they will leave the madness." He turned to each of us and raised his eyebrows in question. "Who would not choose Light over madness?"

The silence that followed gave us time to consider their words. Will there always be those who choose madness over Light? Leonard, for instance. When someone is so damaged by their childhood is there any possibility for them to leave their darkness? Emily stirred and stretched with a big yawn and Grandmother, squinting, looked up toward the sun. "Be maybe time for lunch?" she suggested, knowing our human appetites.

Walt stood, lifting Emily in his arms and said with excitement and a glimmer of mischief, "Ah, yes! Let us take joy in this time. We shall have a feast!"

We began to walk toward the house but stopped when we realized that Walt and Grandmother were still standing in the meadow. "Aren't you coming with us," Shelly asked, shading her eyes from the sun.

We waited but he only lowered Emily to the ground where she stood looking up at him. He raised his arms, closed his eyes and threw back his head and there in the meadow was a shadow-change. Shimmering, it came into colors then faded...emerging, clearer, clearer, awakening hues vibrating with becoming. I began to recognize what was progressing into form as the colors intensified then solidified.

My friends stood as awestruck as I. We had witnessed so much in these past months, experienced things not of this earth, yet it seemed these things would never cease to leave us breathless. Grandmother observed us and smiled at our amazement for she knew that what always seemed like miracles to us was just the Way things were.

Out of seemingly nothing, out of nowhere Walt had crystallized a gift for us. A long table stood on the grass, a spotless white cloth upon it and a feast so magnificent it was a work of art. Lowering his arms, he sang out in his rich, warm voice, "Come, come! I have prepared a table before you!" Then he laughed, full melodious sounds that rose out of the joy in him.

We approached the table, not daring to touch anything as if this were simply too beautiful to disturb for to take one thing from this manifestation seemed like defacing an artist's masterpiece.

"Oh, Walt!" I sighed, blinking in astonishment, "It's so beautiful." I touched one finger to a bowl of the most sumptuous fruit I had ever seen, to convince myself it was real.

"It is my pleasure to give you all," he answered. Then he swung Emily up into his arms and danced through the meadow, Emily's squeals of delight blending with his singing. Their dance took them to the edge of the meadow where the woods began, then back again. Jubilant birds circled them, following, dipping and diving over the clovered field. He chuckled merrily, his eyes twinkling. "You see the abundance before you upon one table and it amazes you. Yet, every spring," he turned a full circle, one arm outstretched to our surroundings, "there is...*this*!" He uttered the word "this" with a gasp. "This that appears all over my earth, a bounty beyond comprehension yet most barely see it."

He lifted a glass of sparkling juice from the table, raised his head back and drank deeply. "Yes," he said with a satisfied sigh, "is life not fine indeed?"

Emily tugged on Walt's sleeve and asked, "Will you sit with me at the picnic?"

"Oh, by all means, Emily! Come, I will fill a plate for us and we can sit together on this lovely grass and tell each other stories."

Shelly and I sat together where the daffodils grew, overwhelmed by the luxurious feast our old friend had provided, moved almost to tears. Words cannot tell of the rare aromas, colors and tastes we were experiencing for this food was never touched by pollution or pesticides. We were eating from the innocence of the mythical Eden, from the untarnished, pure essence of life itself. The fruits, fat and unblemished, seemed to pulse with energy and vitality and when put into our mouths, juices running down our chins, felt as though they had an *intent* to merge with us, to flow in our bloodstreams and seek out our tissues. I felt a deep gratefulness in my heart and wondered it this was what is called "grace."

I observed the scene before me—Emily perched on the nest of Walt's lap, his cheek close to hers as he held a peach to her mouth which she daintily nibbled. Grandmother was feeding tiny pieces of cheese to Jake while she spoke quietly with Dorothy and Robert. Jeff, Don and George sat together discussing ways of natural farming and composting so that all food grown would taste like that which had been provided by Walt. Behind them stood our Maypole, the breeze tugging at the colorful ribbons as if trying to free them from where they'd been entwined.

The sky over the sun-dappled meadow was cerulean blue with occasional puffy white clouds and birds soared as if to some orchestral harmony audible only to them. Pine, birch, maple and oak trees surrounding the meadow, their branches heavy with new leaves, swayed gently to the same harmony. I was content in that fragrant and musical place. A dream? Or was this the way life was meant to be lived? Was this the way food was meant to taste, the way the air originally smelled, the true way of love and friendship?

The day passed in a glorious dream and the sun was lowering, creating long deep shadows layering beside luminous golden sun patches. The air cooled and felt moister, bringing forth the fragrance of the earth. Birds began their afternoon's chorus, circling in the sky in energetic activity before nightfall would confine them to their perches. Bees' humming continued but their fat little bodies were heavy and logy with the cooling temperature.

Grandmother stood, brushed bits of grass from her tunic and we waited to see if something was required of us. She and Walt began to walk down the path to the woods where the ceremonial grounds waited. We followed, walking under the archway of heavy limbs and when we came to the site that George, Shelly and Don had prepared earlier, Walt touched a match to the dried leaves and soon a fire was crackling within the small circle of stones. As before, our clearing in the woods was filled with enchantment: wind chimes, ribbons and candles. We sat, holding our hands to the fire for the coming night's air had chilled us. As the sunlight slowly left the forest Shelly lit all the candles surrounding us and the early evening's curtain was drawn around us. Robert began a slow, rhythmical drumming which blended with the delicate tinkling of wind chimes. In the distance came spring's nightly chorus of peepers. Magic was happening.

Walt began a deep chanting that seemed to emanate from my bones and everyone stood and joined the throbbing beat while Grandmother regally lifted her flute, creating the mystical blue light to encircled us. The ground itself felt as though it were pulsating with us, the trees hummed, the crows called out and Mother Earth reached out to encourage.

As the sounds gradually ebbed I opened my eyes and sank to the ground, tingling as if each chakra point in my body were spinning. Our teachers allowed us time to breathe deeply, the buzzing within us waning, our minds returning to a state of being capable of using our ordinary senses. Soon all we could hear was the whispering of the trees, the singing of the peepers and the wind chimes' music.

Bess and Cricket had stirred from whatever sun-filled thicket they'd slept in during the day and, on silent feet, joined our circle. Brother Crow flew out of the dark forest and landed on a pine branch, calling out his presence and eyeing us from above. He swayed from one foot to the other as if impatient for Grandmother and Walt to speak, as if anticipating something momentous.

Grandmother's mouth wrapped around her music as she played her flute softly. The notes seemed to undulate around us as Walt's eyes searched each face. "We have prepared you for this day."

There is was again. Prepared us for what? My stomach tightened, despite all I had learned. Making a conscious effort, I relaxed my muscles, telling myself that "all was as it should be."

Lowering her flute Grandmother smiled at us warmly, assuring us with her eyes that all *was* as it should be. Her voice, when she began speaking, wove around the other night sounds. "You hear singing of whales, you learn of ancient ways, blend of science and magic. You know about balance, you know about Oneness of life. Use lessons well in days to come. Big changes going to start happening. Big change always cause upheaval. When people try so hard to hold onto things, when they be so scared to try better ways to live, that when life be very full of pain for them. Changes act like big wound but wound have to open up, be looked at to be healed.

"For many, many years people be doing stuff to hurt Mother Earth, to hurt selves. Now be time to face all that. It all have to be looked at. No more secrets. It be time to see ancient ways, Native people ways. It be time for seeing that Mother Nature be God, be Goddess. Creator not some man up in sky that make you beg, who keep good stuff from children, who punish children, even. Creator, God, Goddess be everything, be *so much* you not even be able to imagine with brains.

"We show you that *you* be part of God, of Goddess." Her hands gestured around the circle to include each of us. "*Everyone* be part of God, of Goddess. Everyone be mother, be father to everyone else. Everyone be sister, brother of everyone else. Each one be teacher of all, each one be student, too. Day be here when wonderful thing happen."

I held my breath. The dream I had so long ago filled my head, the dream in which Grandmother gave me the urn and said, "When this be filled with your tears you be ready to enter kingdom of heaven." I had asked her, "But, Grandmother, what about laughter?" She had replied, "Laughter can not be contained." Were the days to come the ones of tears or of laughter?

The next words she spoke echoed in my head and took my breath away.

"This be last time you *see* Grandmother and Walt."

"No!" I protested, shaking my head. The others in our circle had the same reaction. I heard the fear in my voice but could not stop the words. "*We love you!*"

She took me in her arms to console me. "You know Grandmother and Walt love you too but you not seem to understand sometime we be telling you all along."

I sat back, wiping the tears from my eyes noticing that all my friends were reacting the same as I. They sat around our beloved teachers, faces sad and anxious. I couldn't speak. My lips trembled as I waited for her to continue.

"Remember how many times you feel alone and we tell you that we always be with you? Hmmm? We say that because that be *truth*! It be truth for everyone. We tell you when we first come to you that we come in human form, we come like this so we be able to sit and talk with you, be friends and teachers. Walt say he always been with you, he be closer than your breath. He say, 'I am within you, your very soul.' He say that and he show you that he be All...he be woman, man, all creatures, all nations, all colors, all races. Viviane tell you, 'I be your wisdom.'

"You not see?" She waited. "We be Light. Light be in you." She paused before she whispered, "*We be in you.*"

I was struggling to understand but what she seemed to be inferring was a nameless, strange concept. My tears continued, partly in fear, partly in joy.

Walt stood, his hair wild around his face, seemed spun from moonlight. His voice enfolded me protectively. "I am God within you. This is no mere metaphor."

Grandmother stood and said, "I be Goddess within you. Look to neighbor and there be God, there be Goddess also."

Their voices seemed to blend, to echo and resonate within me. "Look to every living creature for there you will see the living breath of the Divine. Your hearts beat together, one cadence, the throbbing of all life."

Grandmother laughed, an almost soundless laugh, like the tinkling of crystal wind chimes. Her radiance broke over us, warm and gold. She stood still, scarcely breathing, her arms extended and her face turned to Walt. The wind picked up and began to howl. Its language was one of endings and beginnings, of dark secrets. It spoke of tales spun out on long winter nights, nights when wind would cry to come in and listen. The wind would hear and when it left it would whisper the tales to others.

Side by side they stood, shoulder to shoulder, a marriage of all living things. Moon above, hung from its vast height, was edged with fire and it seemed to float free from its orbit, running like liquid gold upon these two. Evensong of birdcall, like a cathedral's vespers, filled the air with the music of ecstasy, wordless poetry. I heard the words of the old Sage, Walt Whitman: "Do you see, O my brothers and sisters? It is not chaos or death...it is form, union, plan. It is eternal life. It is happiness."

These forms that love had woven around itself, as Walt, as Grandmother, stood solid before our eyes but then began to waver, as heat-waves over the sun's desert sand. We, in our awed humanity, reached out for them and our awakening divinity hesitantly opened. The body of Walt began to interweave with that of the Grandmother and they merged, one to the other, as transparencies overlapping, becoming one. The voice of both spoke now as one harmonious sound.

"Now you know. *We are you.* We are the male, we are the female, closer than your own hearts, closer than your breath. Never again will you feel alone for all you need do is turn inward. Oh so long ago it was told to you—within you is the Kingdom."

I sighed deeply, my breath a cradle's rhythm rocking me in Mother Earth's arms. The Light that they were flowed into us and meshed with us. Their Light *was us* and laughed within our being. We heard their last whispered words soothing softly like wind in trees, like a lullaby:

Live! Live every moment knowing all is sacred.
Ride upon the wave of limitless love and believe...
Believe, in warm and tender joy,
That you, wondrous child, are a miracle...a miracle...a miracle...

René Donovan

The Gateway

The Beings of mystery,
Mother, Father, Friend
Whisper within us
Of timelessness,
Of spacelessness,
Of unrealized divinity.
It whispers, "I am."
It whispers, "It has begun."
The eye opens.

René Donovan

Amazon Reviews
Me 'n God in the Coffee Shop

*****A magical journey of discovery that each of us is a miracle
Pamela Blevins, Music Historian, Arlington, Virginia on April 25, 1998

An irresistible title coupled with a cover of infinite brilliance (you'll know what I mean when you see it) mark the beginning of a marvelous journey for readers of René Donovan's novel "Me 'n God in the Coffee Shop." Set in a small New England town,"Me'n God in the Coffee Shop" is both lighthearted and serious, a gentle yet thought-provoking and thoroughly enjoyable look at life's possibilities IF only we would permit ourselves to be open to them. René Donovan reveals herself to be a gifted story teller who has created a special world on the pages of this compelling book. I came away from meeting Walt, Grandmother and a host of other fascinating and enchanting characters knowing that the world does not need to be the indifferent, selfish and angry place its seems to have become. What René Donovan conveyed to me, and what she will convey to everyone who reads her insightful book, is that each of us has the power within to shine a positive light on our world and make it a place where peace, harmony and love prevail. And readers will learn something vitally important about themselves in the process -- that each of us is a miracle!! "Me 'n God in the Coffee Shop" is magical, enriching and enlightening, one of those rare books that not only tells a good story but one that can also change how we think and how we live -- all for the better. It is a moving and powerful book that should be on everyone's "Must Read" list.

*****A gentle, yet powerful tale, of magic, miracles and hope!
May 2, 1998

This book is about magic and miracles...and the surprising discovery of where to look for them. A message of hope and empowerment, delivered in the unlikely context of a coffee shop. Donovan's characters draw the reader into an intriguing search for understanding and meaning in a world so fraught with problems. In a society struggling with decadence, violence, intolerance and apathy...Donovan offers an uplifting alternative. She leads the reader on a journey resulting in the joyful affirmation of our oneness with the earth, the universe and all living things. A gentle, yet powerful tale, the author truly provides each reader with a gift...hope!

*****Makes me want to order a "cuppa" & see what happens!
M. Pamela Sekula
(Cohocton, New York United States), May 3, 1998

Renè Donovan weaves a wonderful spell around the reader and her characters. Reminiscent of ancient teachers and mythology, she unfolds Nature's side of religion and philosophy in a warm homey way. I felt like brewing a cup of hazelnut coffee and snuggling into a big chair to join Diane, Shelly and "Walt." ("A Circle of Stones" by Judith Duerk affected me that way.) Well worth the read!

*****Straight from the Cosmos!
May 18, 1998

Ms. Donovan's story is so entertaining that it's almost possible to miss The Truth contained in *Me 'n God in the Coffee Shop*...but not quite. Truth back lights the tale, bringing gems of light to live by. Happily, the underlying good vs. evil theme arrives not from the pulpit, but straight from the Heart of the Cosmos (the easier to see you with, my dear).

***A fun read, and thought provoking to boot!
November 17, 1998

This delightful book was an easy read, yet the unique approach to spirituality kept me thinking, even reexamining the way we think about "god." The plot and commentary push open the mind's windows and let some new light in, and like a draught of fresh air, rejuvenates the mind.

*****A sparkling tale to make your heart sing
By Seamus Drew on December 25, 1999

René Donovan's sparkling descriptions of nature and the miracles of everyday life make my heart sing. It's good to know that I'm not alone in seeing God's glory in every ounce of creation. As I write this review on a north bound flight, the Canadian Rockies glisten outside my window in snowy majesty, their silent voices proclaiming, "She's right you know! There's joy and beauty in all of God's handiwork."
Though everyone may not agree with the beliefs and practices described in this book, the principles of love and divinity set forth are universal. Whether you embrace the Pentacle or the Cross, after reading *Me 'n God in the Coffee Shop* you must agree that God is love no matter by what name we might call him. The author has done a marvelous job of conveying meaningful concepts through the medium of fiction.

*****Magic, miracles and the smell of great coffee...
January 27, 1999

Renè Donovan offers her readers more than a great story: she gives the gift of the divine. Love flows from every page, love of self, love of the Earth, and love for the divine that exists in all. For those on a path of spiritual awakening, the book offers encouragement and reaffirmation. Those who have not yet stepped on the path may well stumble onto it through this incredibly wise, funny, and uplifting tale. It is rare to encounter the divine in everyday life; rarer still to run across it in a novel. But *"Me 'n God in the Coffee Shop"* is most certainly a divinely inspired work, refreshing in its hopeful outlook and its wonderful message that "each of us is a miracle." Spiritual seekers will love this book, and Starbucks should, too...

*****A Thrilling Experience
Maura Rand on January 4, 2000

I loved the God in *Me 'n God in the Coffee Shop* that Donovan portrayed. So caring, loving and real. I was right there, breathlessly waiting for each new encounter. I talked with Grandma for months after finishing the book. A very moving tribute to a new author. I can't wait for her next book.

*****A book to read again and again
Jana Ashba (Wapakoneta, ohio, US) - August 16, 2014

I cherish the day that *Me 'n God in the Coffee Shop* came into my hands. I began this journey of words and very soon it became "the book I couldn't put down." Truth is, Renè Donovan's characters, Walt and Grandmother are now a real part of my life. I reread the book yearly as the season turns to fall, in order to savor the life wisdom offered within. I laugh aloud as the storyteller, Diana, tries to explain to herself the appearance of these two entities that have entered her life. This book boosts my spirit and feeds my sense of what God is, and is certainly my soul's Church. The author, through the words of Walt and Grandmother, reminds us that "We Are the Light." *Me 'n God in the Coffee Shop"* may be a work of fiction, but it's brimming with truths to live by. This book is magical!

René Donovan

Also by
Renè Donovan

The Daughters of Time

On a summer afternoon in 1998, Lizzie Chetwyrd embarks on a journey that will change her life, and the world, forever.

Lizzie's journeys begin through a fold in time—to 1842 where she meets her great-great-great-great Grandmother Sophronia. She befriends the visionaries Emerson and Thoreau who soon suspect that she is more than a visiting relative. As the friendship deepens between Lizzie and the writers, they learn of her otherworldly journeys. Emerson's writing begin to reflect Lizzie's experience and his growing belief that—"Time and space are just inverse measures of the force of the soul. A man is capable of abolishing them both. The spirit sports with time."

The Stone Children

The Stone Children opens at the end of World War ll in Germany. Uriel, a young soldier among those liberating Buchenwald Concentration Camp, sees not only the horrors but also sees images of butterflies, the symbol of transformation, drawn on the floors and walls of the barracks by children who had been imprisoned there. He learns that these images are in every camp and is deeply affected.

When the war in the Pacific ends Uriel returns to his Cape Cod village, marries his childhood sweetheart Marra and begins his career as a children's book illustrator. Their home is filled with love but Uriel's nights are tortured by nightmares of the horrors he witnessed at Buchenwald. Marra, a sculptor, also begins to dream. She dreams of eggs. She dreams of children:

Eggs, at first. Her dreams swam with the images of smooth-shelled eggs: brown, white, blue, speckled. From deep within the eggs came songs as if their interiors held choirs. She felt the sound in her belly like something growing inside her, something that wanted to be born into the world.

A force had entered Uriel at Buchenwald, a *something* that wants to be known. It wants to communicate through him and Marra, guiding their art and bearing a healing message for all humanity. It wants to prepare the world for the children to come, the *Lumins,* the compassionate children who had died in the Holocaust.

This story takes the reader from World War ll through all the years that followed up to the infamous morning of September 11, 2001. Intertwined amid the turmoil and confusion of those years are wonders and changes that raise humanity's awareness. *"There is a noble fragment within us, a kind of beginning, a small secret...coiled love in fluid stone."*

www.ingramcontent.com/pod-product-compliance
Lightning Source LLC
LaVergne TN
LVHW051829080426
835512LV00018B/2787